KHA
&
THE CROWN PRINCE

KHASHOGGI
&
THE CROWN PRINCE

THE SECRET FILES

by

Oliver Wilson

GIBSON SQUARE

This edition published for the first time by Gibson Square in 2019

UK   Tel: +44 (0)20 7096 1100
US   Tel: +1 646 216 9813

     rights@gibsonsquare.com
     www.gibsonsquare.com

     ISBN 978-1-78334-069-9

Printed by Clays.

INDEX

The Secret Files

ৡ

Mohammed bin Salman, the Crown Prince of Saudi Arabia or, more popularly, 'MBS', used to be of interest only to dedicated Kingdom watchers. He had only popped on the global-news radar a few of times since his appointment on 21 June 2017 – once for imprisoning his relatives in a five-star hotel for a shake-down to fill the royal coffers, and another time for kidnapping the Lebanese Prime Minister Saad al-Hariri and having him beaten. He seemed a colourful, feisty character who didn't hesitate to pick on people his own size. And then he was also in the news for glad-handing Silicon-valley moguls keen to associate with him.

Yet this relatively low-key profile changed abruptly in the first week of October 2018 when he suddenly had the international-media spell-bound following a continuous news murder-mystery akin to the dramatic hunt for Saddam Hussein and Muammar Gaddafi. Astonishingly, it was his fellow Sunni-Muslim leader, the Turkish President Recep Erdoğan, who launched the opening shot on 6 October. On that day Turkish officials leaked to the press a blunt statement that a Saudi commoner had been murdered on 2 October in the Saudi Embassy in Istanbul. The news ran as a thunder bolt through the global media.

On that day, Jamal Khashoggi, a Saudi national

resident in the US in his early sixties, had flown into Istanbul from London – where he had attended a conference and had dinner in a restaurant (just around the corner from where I live) – in order to obtain a marriage license in the Saudi-Arabian consulate in Istanbul.

Although a commoner and not a royal, Khashoggi belonged to the highest echelons of the Saudi elite that surrounded and served the Saudi royal family. He had started his career as a bookseller and journalist, but by birth he was closely related to the pre-eminent Saudi arms dealer and billionaire Adnan Khashoggi, while Jamal's grandfather was the private physician to the first King Saud. He was also related to billionaire and former Harrod's owner Mohammed al-Fayed son Dodi, who died with Princess Diana in Paris.

Even more significantly, Khashoggi, had been advisor to Prince Turki al-Faisal when he was Saudi Ambassador to the United Kingdom, 2003-5, and to the United States, 2005-7. They had had a long working relationship on Saudi secrets well before that. During Prince Turki's uninterrupted 22-year reign as head of Saudi intelligence they had worked closely together. While Khashoggi's uncle Adnan sold guns to the Afghans (doubtless paid for by the Saudis and Americans) to fight Soviet Russia, Khashoggi himself had been the secret Saudi liaison to Osama bin Laden – then still the good guy fighting Russia and not the founder of al-Qaeda.

On 2 October Khashoggi's fiancée had alerted *Washington Post* Istanbul bureau chief Kareem Fahim that Khashoggi had mysteriously disappeared after visiting the Saudi embassy in Istanbul, who duly posted an item on his blog from London.

It wasn't much of a news story yet and no one paid much attention. But the allegation that Saudi Arabia's *de facto* leader Prince bin Salman – known to the security agencies as MBS – had sent a hit squad to Turkey to dispose of a member of the Saudi secret-intelligence community instantly circulated among se services around the world. Clearly, the CIA, MI6, and the security services of Turkey and Saudi Arabia – not to mention Russia's FSB and GRU, Mossad, France's Deuxième Bureau, Germany's BND and the intelligence services of other countries that sold arms to Saudi Arabia – took a keen interest and began amassing secret files for their governments.

These top-secret files stayed hermetically shut, however, to prying eyes that might cause unwanted turbulence by casting light on the facts of the mater. Only highly specialised intelligence branches of government have the capability to piece facts together and the experts are bound to complete secrecy by government contracts and criminal law, if not professional pride alone. Many of the ways of gathering this intelligence would be considered illegal in any case. Unless a government had a particular agenda it wanted to achieve, the information in these files would remain under lock and key.

There was no chance that the media would find out more either on its own as it had in the cases of the excruciating deaths of Alexander Litvinenko from Polonium 210 poisoning in 2006 or Dawn Sturgess's after the poisoning of Sergei Skripal with a top-secret Soviet nerve agent in 2018.

Turkey and, even more so, Saudi Arabia are hermetically shut to a free press trying to dig around sensitive subjects. Both countries – like Russia or China, or, for that matter, the world's other authoritarian regimes – have draconic ways of deterring infractions – whether by a journalist or not – by those who show too much interest in matters that might compromise the state.

Without a free press being able to do their own investigation, Khashoggi's enigmatic disappearance would soon be filed away as a loose end rather than a red-hot developing news story. Indeed, given Khashoggi's measure of criticism of Saudi Arabia in his writings and his last sighting at the Saudi consulate, all that could be said, in the absence of hard facts about the disappearance, was that that this mystery looked like yet another instance of the suppression of dissent by a totalitarian regime.

Yet 4 days after Khashoggi's disappearance, instead of vanishing into a news fog, something remarkable happened to the story.

After initially seeming as bemused as anyone, it was the Turkish government that suddenly lit the blue touch paper on 6 October when the two officials leaked their blunt message to the *Washington Post* that 'Mr Khashoggi has been killed at the consulate,' and, just to twist the knife, the anonymous officials added 'We believe that the murder was premeditated and the body was subsequently moved out of the consulate.'

The accusation of premeditated immediately brought Khashoggi and the Crown Prince to the attention of the world. Particularly as the day after the alleged death of Khashoggi, no less a person than the Crown Prince himself had protested innocence of Khashoggi's whereabouts. 'We have nothing to hide' he had said in a Bloomberg blog interview on the evening of 3 October.

Not known for their love of the free media, the Turkish government subsequently started to leak a steady and grisly stream of detailed information about the events in the Saudi consulate. These nuggets of information started to shape a new reputation of the Crown Prince of Saudi Arabia as a ghoulish potentate in the mould of Vladimir Putin, Saddam Hussain, the Assads.

Fanning the flames further, President Erdoğan signalled in a number of personal statements that he would not stop until he had achieved his objective – whatever that was exactly. Erdoğan (despite his own gloves-off vendetta against over-inquisitive journalists), for example, wrote an opinion piece in the *Washington Post* on the matter, and called the murder 'savage' and 'planned' in press conferences. The kingdom still pretended it had no idea what had happened to Khashoggi, but the Turkish drip feed would prove irresistible to keep MBS and Khashoggi's assassination in the spotlight.

In the age of blogs, tweets, Wikileaks and online diplomacy, it was now in the interests of all nations involved strategically to assess, like Turkey had, whether to leak their own information where this made sense for political and commercial gain.

Spooks these days do not go around breaking into safes and photographing top-secret documents with miniature cameras to file away in top-secret folders at their end for her majesty's eyes only. Instead they comb the internet, hack emails, copy CCTV footage and piece together other scraps of information they can lay their hands to answer the questions that remain in a complex jigsaw puzzle of national and private interests: what did Khashoggi know that made it imperative that he was killed, how is it connected to President Trump; why is Turkey taking such aim at the kingdom, given that the Crown Prince in some ways uses Turkey as a model for reform; how does it relate to Qatar, where the US has its largest base in the Middle East, Iran, Israel etc?

Every single fact that we know about the Khashoggi case derives entirely from these secret files. This book aims to reconstruct what was in them. Unlike the days before the internet, this reconstruction is now eminently possible. Khashoggi's Barbaric assassination has pulled away the curtain in one fell swoop from the secretive world of Middle-Eastern power play and not just the fateful and grisly intertwining of the fate of the two men at the heart of it.

1
Istanbul

ॐ

A private jet with tail markings HZ-SK1 touched down at Istanbul's Atatürk Airport at 3.13am on 2 October 2018. It had come from Riyadh, the capital of Saudi Arabia. Nine people arrived on this flight. They were members of the Saudi security forces and checked into two Istanbul hotels – the Mövenpick Hotel and the Wyndham Grand where they were caught on in-house cameras passing through security and checking in. From the top-floor windows, the men could almost see the nearby Saudi Arabian consulate, which was tucked away in a quiet street in an Istanbul financial district. Both hotels are just a short drive away.

Although Saudi Arabia is immensely wealthy from oil money, its consulate in Istanbul is far from impressive. Overshadowed by the towers of Istanbul's Levent business district, it is a far cry from the modern Saudi Arabia dreamt of by its powerful Crown Prince Mohammed bin Salman with his vision of skyscraper cities in the desert. Behind security barriers and razor wire, the consulate is more Fawlty Towers and has the air of a shabby 1970s office building. The ceilings are low and the corridors are harshly lit. Telephone calls are often put through to the wrong person. On the desks, shambolic stacks of paper wait to be rubber-stamped, sometimes spilling onto the floor in a jumble of passport photos and visa applications. It is also an unlikely murder scene.

Saudi Arabian writer and intelligence insider Jamal Khashoggi, a fifty-nine-year-old columnist for the *Washington Post* and a prominent critic of Crown Prince Mohammed bin Salman, arrived at the consulate at 1.14pm. In self-imposed exile in Virginia, he needed copies of divorce papers prior to this forthcoming marriage to a fourth wife. She was a Turkish national. Consequently he had been directed to pick up the paperwork in Istanbul by MBS's brother, Prince Khalid bin Salman bin Abdulaziz al-Saud, the Saudi ambassador in Washington, DC. Arranging to collect the documents in Istanbul, he had been assured that he would be safe. He had visited the consulate on Friday, 28 September 2018, but the divorce papers were not ready and he was told to return the following Tuesday, 2 October. Khashoggi flew to London to attend a conference and stayed there for the weekend, returning to the consulate on Tuesday afternoon. He never left.

The Saudis had had four days to plan how to get rid of Jamal Khashoggi, who was a close friend to high-ranking members of the Saudi royal family and significant enough to be known personally to Crown Prince bin Salman. Sensing that there might be trouble, despite assurances to the contrary, Khashoggi himself was accompanied by his thirty-six-year-old fiancée Hatice Cengiz, a PhD student at university in Istanbul. She especially took a day off class to be with him. She was to wait outside the consulate. He gave her his mobile phone before he went in. If anything went wrong and he did not emerge in an hour, she was to call a friend, a fellow who was an advisor to President Erdoğan himself.

Khashoggi had reason to be careful. Despite his place in the rarefied Saudi corridors of power, in the late summer of 2017 he had gone into self-imposed exile following a ban from public speaking imposed on him by Saudi Arabia's government. Remarkably, this ban had little to do with any criticism Khashoggi might have of Saudi politics, but rather with his criticism of president-elect Donald Trump as 'contradictory' at an obscure energy conference at The Washington Institute, a think tank, two days after Trump had won the election in 2016. The Saudi government, presumably, saw the vain and volatile billionaire and soon-to-be president as their mark and feared Khashoggi's views might be seen as those among the royal elite. Or, perhaps, it was the fact that Khashoggi had commented on Trump's closeness to Russia. Stung like a bee, Saudi Arabia had issued an official press release: 'The author Jamal Khashoggi does not represent the government of Saudi Arabia or its positions at any level'.

While in US exile in Virginia, Khashoggi had started writing regular columns for the *Washington Post*. In his first one he wrote, 'I have left my home, my family and my job, and I am raising my voice. To do otherwise would betray those who languish in prison. I can speak when so many cannot. I want you to know that Saudi Arabia has not always been as it is now. We Saudis deserve better.' He also had his own Twitter account, written in Arabic, with 2 million followers. On the whole his *Post* columns were but mildly critical of the desert-kingdom's new policies, and indeed occasionally laudatory, though he had also used his column to comment on the Crown Prince, the most powerful man in the oil-rich kingdom after King Salman. He had also continued to criticise Donald Trump by name, lastly in his column of 28 August 2018 on the Muslim Brotherhood, for not correcting 'Obama's mistakes.'

When the door was closed behind him, Khashoggi was ushered to the second floor of the building and into the office of the consul general. This would have befitted someone of Khashoggi's status in Saudi society. He was a man who had advised senior royals, including the former ambassador to London and Washington, and intelligence chief, Prince Turki, and the ruler of Saudi Arabia until 2015, King Abdullah.

Khashoggi should have had little reason to fear consul general Mohammed al-Otaibi as he sat down in a guest chair opposite his desk. The consul general had personally called him and invited him back to finalise his papers, after the failed attempt the previous Friday.

Khashoggi, however, was not the only stranger in the building. A large elite squad of military had been waiting for him, all members of the state's security apparatus who had arrived earlier in the morning. The hit squad, which had flown in from Riyadh on charters and scheduled flights, some ten hours earlier was drawn from the most elite units of the Saudi security forces. Their fidelity had been repeatedly tested in previous assignments. Among them were major general Maher Abdulaziz Mutreb, an officer who was attached to the Crown Prince's security detail and well-known to Khashoggi, and Dr Salah Muhammed al-Tubaigy, the head of forensics in the kingdom's interior ministry. Mutreb and his team had been filmed by a security camera outside the consulate walking towards the door.

Turkish employees of the consulate had unexpect-edly been given the afternoon off on 2 October. Sent home before noon they had been told that an important diplomatic delegation was arriving for a meeting. The loyalties of the Saudis remaining in the building could not be questioned.

It was a simple matter to disable the consulate's CCTV. Any record of what happened behind the building's walls would be taken back to Saudi Arabia. What was about to take place there would never be known to the outside world. Or so the elite Saudi death squad thought.

But in Turkey, and elsewhere, diplomatic missions sometimes have ears. Unbeknownst to the Saudis, intelligence officials from at least one national spy agency were listening in and hearing every sound and every word spoken during their operation. Just which spy agency and how they managed to get their recording has been the subject of much intrigue throughout intelligence agencies around the world.

Not long after Khashoggi entered the consul's office, major general Mutreb entered with three other members of the death squad.

Surprised to see the familiar face of his former London-embassy colleague, Khashoggi asked what Mutreb was doing here. Mutreb told him curtly that he had to return to Saudi Arabia. Khashoggi refused. There followed seven minutes of quarrelling during which Khashoggi shouted, 'Release my arm! What do you think you are doing?' At the same time, there was a heated Skype call to Saud al-Qahtani, one of the Crown Prince's closest advisors known in dissident circles as the 'Saudi Steve Bannon'.

Khashoggi also knew al-Qahtani well. A month after leaving Saudi in 2017, al-Qahtani had called him in Virginia and given praise for his support for the Crown Prince's decision to let women drive. 'Keep writing and boasting', al-Qahtani had added unctuously. This time, al-Qahtani dropped all pretence of charm. Khashoggi was told he was being kidnapped and would be taken back to Saudi Arabia by force.

'You can't do that,' Khashoggi replied fearfully, 'People are waiting outside.' 'People' was a generous term. He was counting on his fiancée to raise the alarm and contact President Erdoğan's advisor as well as the Turkish authorities if she saw anything suspicious.

During the following seven horrific minutes, the four men beat and tortured him. Consul general Otaibi asked them to do this outside, fearing that it would get him into trouble. He was told to shut up if he wanted to live when he returned to Saudi Arabia. Meanwhile Khashoggi repeatedly pleaded, 'I can't breathe'. These would be the last words he ever spoke.

Jamal Khashoggi's grisly fate was played out behind closed doors in a secure building – in a diplomatic mission which is a piece of sovereign territory where the host nation and others are not supposed to pry.

Yet the information about Khashoggi's macabre fate would come exclusively, from 'sources'. That is people who prefer to remain anonymous within the governments of Turkey, Saudi Arabia, Russia, the US, the UK, France, Germany and others, each of whom were towing their own self-interest in leaking the information to the international media. Facts would not be coming from independent press investigations, as it would in countries with a free press.

Some two hours after Khashoggi had entered the consulate, six vehicles left. Two arrived at the residence of Mohammed al-Otaibi, the Saudi consul general who lived five hundred yards away at 3.09pm. It was an imposing building crowned with the Saudi emblem of golden crossed swords and a palm tree. A Saudi flag flew outside. Here too Turkish employees at the residence had hastily been told to immediately to take the day off. One of the vehicles, a Mercedes Vito van with tinted windows, pulled into the garage there. Neighbours of the consul general's residence, which is situated next to a popular restaurant, reported that for the first time ever there had been a barbecue that afternoon next to the pool in the large fenced-in garden of the residence. The neighbours had speculated what the barbecue was for, it was reported.

At 6.20pm the second jet took off heading for Cairo. After spending twenty-five hours on the ground there, it flew on to Riyadh. The Saudi men from the first flight were seen leaving their hotels around 8pm that evening. The first plane left Istanbul at 10.35pm. It made a stop about 170 miles to the east in Nallihan, Turkey. It then skirted the border between Iraq and Iran, favouring the Iraqi side, and crossed the Persian Gulf, landing in Dubai at 2.30am. The following morning, it flew on to Riyadh. Thirteen passengers departed on these flights – six in one group, seven in the second.

Khashoggi's fiancée had left waiting outside the consulate which closed at 3.30p. At 4pm, she alerted the Turkish authorities. She was still seen waiting outside the consulate forlornly at 5.33pm. Neither she, nor anyone else, would ever see Jamal Khashoggi alive again.

The disappearance of the high-ranking writer had, in principle, been pulled off like clock-work by a practised team of highly skilled men. The Saudis were adept at disappearing people and no more should have been heard of it.

Then everything began to go wrong, not least of all for the man who ordered the assassination.

2

The Crown Prince

૭

Until the murder of Jamal Khashoggi, Crown Prince
Mohammed bin Salman or MBS had been the darling
of the West where he was seen by pundits and
governments alike as a desperately-needed reformer
in a country stuck in the Middle Ages and run in
increasingly geriatric succession by the sons of King
Ibn Saud. MBS had opened cinemas and restricted
the powers of the religious police. Women were
allowed to drive and visit sports stadiums. The first
public concert featuring a female singer had been
held. His shakedown of the starchy generation of
older princes was understandable as the Kingdom
was suffering from the low oil prices.

Dynamic MBS planned to diversify the economy,
moving Saudi Arabia away from its slavish
dependence on oil. He also spent an awful lot of
money buying Western arms. Tantalisingly, he also
toyed with idea of privatising the state oil company
Saudi Aramco, the world's most profitable company,
in order the plug the gaping hole in the royal coffers
of the desert kingdom. Although it would only be 5%
of the company, the West (that is US oil companies
Texaco, Exxon, Mobil) had been excluded from
owning part of the company ever since nationalisa-
tion in the seventies.

But by the normal rules, MBS should not have

been in a position of power at all. Saudi Arabia was founded in 1932 under King Ibn Saud. After he died in 1953, he was supposed to be succeeded in turn by all his surviving sons (he had forty five at the time of his death, thirty six of whom survived their father) and six of them would indeed become king. When the sixth one, King Salman, ascended the throne in 2015, his younger brother the septuagenarian Prince Muqrin duly became the next Crown Prince and First Deputy Prime Minister. But after just three months, King Salman replaced him with his nephew Prince bin Nayef, making him first in line to the throne. However, in June 2017, this prince was also sacked by royal decree and replaced by Salman's own son Mohammed bin Salman or MBS.

Born in 1985, MBS was the eldest child of King Salman's third wife Fahda bint Falah bin Sultan bin Hathleen. Several of King Salman's other sons, who studied overseas to perfect foreign languages and earn advanced degrees, built impressive résumés. One became the first Arab astronaut, another a deputy oil minister, yet another the governor of Medina Province.

But MBS stayed in Saudi Arabia and does not speak English fluently, although he appears to understand it. Rachid Sekkai, who taught him English and later worked for the BBC, said he toyed with a walkie-talkie in class and was more interested in playing in the garden and cracking jokes with his brothers and the guards. When the chance came to visit America, he refused to go to the US Embassy for a visa, to be finger-printed 'like some criminal', according to a State Department cable.

While his father was still governor of Riyadh Province, MBS was brought up in a palace that was built like a fortress. After a private education, he studied law at King Saud University in Riyadh, graduating fourth in his class. Another prince of the same generation said he had gotten to know him during high school when one of their uncles held regular dinners for the younger princes at his palace. He recalled MBS being one of the crowd, saying he liked to play bridge and admired Margaret Thatcher.

At the age of twenty four, MBS became an advisor to his father prince Salman. Other political appointments followed and when his father became second deputy prime minister and defence minister, MBS remained in post as his father's private advisor. Prince Salman became crown prince in 2012, then king in January 2015, naming MBS as Deputy Crown Prince and minister of defence. This gave him a lot of sway in the West with arms procurements.

It was in his new capacity as minister of defence that MBS first wielded power.

In neighbouring Yemen, the rebel Houthi militia of the Shiite Zaidi sect and forces loyal to the former president Ali Abdullah Saleh, who had been ousted in 2012, took the capital city Sana'a in 21 March 2015 and proclaimed themselves the official government of Yemen. They left Saleh's Sunni successor Abdrabbuh Mansur Hadi in power in the principal port of Aden, however, while Al-Qaeda in the Arabian Peninsula and the Islamic State of Iraq and the Levant also gained control of parts of Yemen. The Houthi then marched on Aden and 'President' Hadi fled on the 25th, finding refuge in Riyadh, where he is understood to be languishing under house arrest.

In retaliation, MBS organised a Sunni coalition of the Gulf states and began air strikes on Houthi positions and imposed a naval blockade. Peremptorily, he did not even bother to inform the head of the National Guard, prince Mutaib din Abdullah, when the first air strikes went in.

Having total command of Yemeni airspace, MBS expected a quick victory over the Houthi and, consequently, the restoration of the Hadi regime which he then could take credit for. At the start of the war, he was often photographed visiting troops and meeting with military leaders. But as the campaign stalemated and dragged on into a war of attrition, his appearances grew rare. When *The Economist* dubbed him the 'architect of the war in Yemen', MBS's response was that he was waging war on Islamic terrorism. As a military leader, MBS had no experience and took frequent holidays, putting himself out of contact for days on end.

Instead of a quick victory, war dragged on and civilian casualties mounted, and MBS drew growing criticism from human rights groups, while diplomats pointed out that the death toll for Saudi troops was higher than the government acknowledged publicly. The prolonged war and the Saudi-led blockade also led to a famine. Half of the war-torn country's population – fourteen million people – were on the brink of starvation and it is estimated that 85,000 children died from malnutrition. (In order to counter these headlines, MBS established the Centre for Studies and Media Affairs to propagate a positive spin on the Yemen war in Washington and he hired numerous Washington lobbying and public relations firms to assist in the PR campaign.)

While oil prices were dropping, MBS paid for the costly war by slashing the state budget, freezing government contracts and reducing the pay of civil employees in the name of austerity. For himself, however, he could not resist buying a 440-foot yacht from a Russian vodka tycoon for $500 million. Fearing assassination with so many enemies, he is said to sleep on board.

He also bought Château Louis XIV near Versailles, France, the world's most expensive home with a $300 million price tag. This modern palace was built by Saudi property developer Emad Khashoggi, a cousin of Jamal. The Leonardo da Vinci painting 'Salvador del Mundo' cost him $450 million in the most expensive art sale in history. And before the murder of Jamal Khashoggi, MBS was planning a £4 billion takeover bid for Manchester United, though the Glazer family said they had no immediate intention of selling the club.

Even before he became crown prince, it quickly became clear that MBS was easing aside Crown Prince bin Nayef who, as long-time counterterrorist prince, had good connections in Washington and the support of many of the older royals. The White House saw an early sign of the ambition of the young prince, however, in late 2015, when – breaking protocol – MBS delivered a soliloquy about the failures of American foreign policy during a meeting between his father King Salman and President Obama.

Given Saudi Arabia's crusty echelons of power and the Saudi crown cascading down aging and infirm brothers, many young Saudis admired MBS as a dynamic representative of their generation who addressed some of the kingdom's problems in a forthright manner. The country's controlled news media lent a helping hand by building up his image as a hardworking, business-like leader less concerned with the trappings of royalty than his predecessors – his profligacy was not covered in the Saudi media. But the old guard among the royal family saw him as a power-hungry inexperienced upstart who didn't understand the consequences of impulsive change.

Early in 2016, the Crown Prince bin Nayef retired to his villa in Algeria. Previously he had taken hunting holidays there, but this time it was different. He stayed away for weeks and was often incommunicado. Even CIA Director John Brennan, who had known him for decades, had trouble reaching him. A diabetic, bin Nayef was also suffering from the prolonged effects of injuries from an assassination attempt where an Al-Qaeda suicide bomber detonated a bomb surgically implanted in his rectum. Bin Nayef was avoiding the predations of MBS, who had his eye on the royal succession.

King Salman had already united his court with that of his son, making MBS Chief of the Royal Court which gave him control of access to the king. King Salman also made MBS head of the lucrative Saudi Aramco, the chief engine of the economy. In addition, MBS himself announced the formation of a military alliance of (Sunni) Islamic countries to fight terrorism. This had long been the province of Prince bin Nayef, but the new alliance gave no role to him or bin Nayef's Interior Ministry. When MBS listed the countries of the alliance, a number of them said they knew nothing about it, or were waiting for information before deciding to join.

In April 2016, MBS launched his ambitious plan for the future of the kingdom, called Vision 2030. This sought to increase employment and improve education, healthcare and other government services.

A National Transformation Plan, laying out targets for improving government ministries, came shortly after. It also called for transparency and accountability, tacitly admitting that they had been missing before.

A luxury beach resort was planned for the Red Sea coast where women would be allowed to wear bikinis in the pool and beach areas. Over $2 billion was invested in an entertainment authority MBS established. This staged live music concerts, comedy shows, wrestling matches and monster truck rallies. A large sports, culture and entertainment complex was to be built, along with a theme park. Meanwhile MBS made continued calls for fiscal responsibility.

Any criticism of the relentless rise of MBS was silenced by phone calls to Saudi journalists telling them they had been barred from publishing, and sometimes from travelling abroad. One Saudi journalist published an article about MBS on his website, the *Riyadh Post*, where he said that the prince's popularity was based on a 'sweeping desire for great change' and the hope that he would 'turn their dreams into reality'. But he said: 'If you fail, this love withers quickly, as if it never existed, and is replaced by a deep feeling of frustration and hatred.' The website was blocked the next day – QED.

Deputy Crown Prince MBS made well-publicised foreign trips to Europe, the Middle East and Washington, where he stayed at the Georgetown home of Secretary of State John Kerry. In September 2015, dinner at Mr Kerry's house ended with Prince bin Salman playing Beethoven on the piano for his host and the other guests. He attended the G20 summit in November 2015, leading commentators to speculate that Crown Prince bin Nayef would be ousted. Then in May 2016, Secretary Kerry was a guest on MBS's yacht, the Serene, and in June 2016, the two men shared an *iftar* dinner, breaking the Ramadan fast.

His influence in Washington was aided by prince Mohammed Bin Zayed al-Nahyan, the Crown Prince of Abu Dhabi and deputy supreme commander of the United Arab Emirates Armed Forces, who was a favourite in the Obama administration and a respected voice in the Sunni world. Both princes shared an innate hostility to Shia Iran and al-Nahyan also had a personal antipathy toward prince bin Nayef.

MBS had to work quickly to establish his power base due to his eighty-one-year-old father's deteriorating health. King Salman had a stroke from which he had not fully recovered before he ascended the throne and was suffering from Alzheimer's. The king had already issued a decree restructuring Saudi Arabia's system for prosecutions that stripped Crown Prince bin Nayef of his long-standing powers of overseeing criminal investigations. Then the king met alone with Crown Prince bin Nayef and asked him to step down, ostensibly because of his addiction to painkilling drugs.

In a final humiliation of bin Nayef, he was forced to pledge loyalty to his successor MBS. He was then under placed under house arrest, while those loyal to him were purged. When MBS became Crown Prince on 21 June 2017, Donald Trump phoned to congratulate him.

In November 2017, MBS made his next move against his aged adversaries. He ordered some two hundred wealthy businessmen, princes and government officials to be detained in Riyadh's palatial Ritz-Carlton hotel. They were only released after they gave up billions of dollars to a new anti-corruption committee set up by the Crown Prince. Bank accounts were frozen and the hotel's internet and telephone lines were disconnected while they remained under house arrest. Those who did not pay up remained in custody. Among those arrested and removed from office was Prince Mutaib bin Abdullah, leader of the Saudi National Guard who enjoyed the support of many fellow princes.

Senior royals meanwhile bitterly complained that MBS used his power as Chief of the Royal Court to curtail their access to King Salman. Ostensibly with the encouragement of his father, MBS then set about restructuring the intelligence agencies, another Saudi power base sceptical of him.

Outside the kingdom, MBS started to throw his

weight around in the first month of his appointment as Crown Prince. He led a blockade of Qatar in 2017, alleging that the Gulf state was supporting Shia terrorism from Iran. Qatar denied this, admitting that it had provided assistance to some Islamist groups such as the Muslim Brotherhood, but not militant groups linked to al-Qaeda or the Islamic State.

Like the war against Shia-governed Yemen, the Qatar blockade has continued, and is only mitigated by imports from Iran, Qatar's neighbour across the Persian Gulf, and Turkey. Turkey's support for Qatar, against Saudi Arabia, marked a sudden chill in the relations between the two nations. Although 70% Sunni, Turkey has both resisted Saudi Wahhabism for centuries and ignored the Shia-Sunni divide in its foreign policy, striking a pragmatic rather than dogmatic course.

Early in 2018, given the gathering headlines against him, MBS decided to brush up his overseas image with a lavish tour projecting a youthful image rather than the usual one in traditional Saudi gold trimmed robes. In the UK, he met Prime Minister Theresa May, Queen Elizabeth and Prince William. Then he flew on to the US where he visited Washington, Hollywood and Silicon Valley, meeting President Trump, Bill and Hillary Clinton, Henry Kissinger, Michael Bloomberg, George W. Bush, George H.W. Bush, Bill Gates, Jeff Bezos, Oprah Winfrey, Rupert Murdoch, Richard Branson, Mayor

Eric Garcetti of Los Angeles, Michael Douglas, Morgan Freeman and Dwayne Johnson. He also met with prominent Jewish groups and garnered almost universal praise.

However, there was one critic writing from the *Washington Post* who sounded a more reserved note – Jamal Khashoggi. Six months later he was dead and world opinion would once again swing against MBS with a vengeance.

3
The 'Traitor'

ꝯ

Jamal Ahmad Khashoggi was in many ways an unlikely dissident. In fact, those who knew him said he was not a dissident at all. He loved his country and, as an exile in the US, he missed his friends and family there if not his life in the highest royal circles. He was at best a lukewarm critic of the kingdom. Before he was forced to flee he had been extremely close to the Saudi regime, even being an advisor to King Salman's predecessor. If anything he was a Saudi grandee and more a writer and commentator than a journalist; and he continued to be privy to secret information through his exceptional contacts and close friendships within the stratosphere of the Saudi royal family.

It was this closeness to Saudi secrets that, together with the criticism of then president-elect Trump, fuelled the theory that he knew something so extremely damaging if not explosive. It was not necessarily just that he had a column in one of Trump-pet figures of hate, the *Washington Post*, and a 2 million Twitter feed. Khashoggi was also a power broker. He had, for example, been given $100,000 on 2 December 2009, when he was advisor to King Abdullah, to help create the elaborate smokescreen of high-level Saudi respectability surrounding the 1DMB, sovereign-wealth fraud. Khashoggi himself wasn't aware of the fraud, but it would ensnare Goldman Sachs with a 6 billion dollar law suit and implode the Malaysian ruling party in 2018, car-crashing its uninterrupted rule since 1957.

Worryingly, Khashoggi seemed on the verge of suddenly creating a new family in Turkey, buying an apartment in Istanbul and nurturing a personal friendship with President Erdoğan, Saudi-Arabia's arch rival for Middle Eastern leadership among Sunni nations. After a year in exile, Khashoggi had become an intelligence liability that had to be neutralised.

The secrets Khashoggi was and had been privy to were on the verge of drifting away from the Saudi sphere of influence into rival territory. He was increasingly seen as a loose end by MBS and his advisors. If his new friends were able to play him – a possibility given that his soon-to-be much younger wife was Turkish – he possessed sensitive information that could fall into the wrong hands.

When Mutreb yelled 'traitor' while his former colleague was being dismembered on video, he dropped an unmistakable clue as to what was really behind the brutal killing.

Khashoggi's importance was not lost either on Vladimir Putin, another world leader who viciously hunted down journalists inside his own country, but who only took lethal aim at intelligence risks beyond Russia's borders.

President Putin would take the opportunity to offer his personal response to the Khashoggi murder on 18

October at a conference in Sochi (the Valdai Discussion Club, Russia's state of the union for top officials and oligarchs). Leaking what was in Russia's intelligence files, he pointedly said about Khashoggi's *curriculum vitae*, 'As far as I can judge this man to a certain extent part of the Saudi elite. In some way or other he was connected to certain circles in power'. Discounting the fact that Khashoggi was also a writer, Putin observed, 'It is hard to say, what is going on there.'

In an even more significant hint of the extent of Russian intelligence, Putin had publicly brought up the subject of 'traitors' on 3 October – the day after the brutal, torture and assassination of Khashoggi, and on the same day on which MBS was to protest publicly and in person his innocence of Khashoggi's fate to Bloomberg in the evening.

Putin was taking part in a midday Q&A sesssion at the Russian Energy Week conference in Moscow, but he had mysteriously veered off the topic into a vitriolic broadside against former-GRU spy Sergei Skripal. It seemed so random at the time that his outburst made the world news. But, speaking at an energy conference, meant that it was in any case guaranteed to be relayed back word for word to Riyadh. Also, seated next to Vladimir Putin at the Q&A session was Khalid al-Failih, MBS's Saudi energy minister and the former CEO of Aramco. He would be able to convey first-hand Putin's passionate view on 'traitors' and what any country should do with them. This message could not have been misunderstood by MBS.

'Imagine' Putin fumed, pulling a disgusted face, 'suddenly someone goes and betrays your country. What do you think about him? ... He's just a scumbag, and that's it.' The Russian word Putin spat out at the conference attended by oil and gas state ministers and CEOs of oil companies was '*poldonok*', a vulgar swear word.

Bizarrely Putin had also added that some 'are pushing forward the theory that Mr Skripal is almost some kind of human rights defender.'

It was an odd straw man to knock down, unless of course the president was talking about a 'traitor' who both possessed national secrets he was taking away from his country as well as being a public defender of human rights. *Washington Post* columnist Jamal Khashoggi, with a two million Twitter feed, could definitely be crowned a human rights defender by the free press. Khashoggi was also a long-standing member of the Saudi intelligence community and privy to secrets of the highest circles of the Saudi royal family and who had been silenced after he spoke out on President Donald Trump. But Sergei Skripal was a retired mid-ranking spy living in very modest circumstances in sleepy Salisbury who had never gone on the record for anything, let alone human rights.

Turkey and the international media still imagined at this point that Khashoggi was alive, but Riyadh knew better. It would not have escaped notice that Putin's words applied within an inch to the events in the Saudi consulate. Not only that, they knew that Putin would high-five their operation.

Few, apart from the Saudi team around MBS, would have guessed at this connection to 'traitor' Jamal Khashoggi. To Western eyes Khashoggi's profile had always looked more far more like that of a writer than that of a power broker who could betray his country as a 'traitor'.

The son of a merchant, Jamal Khashoggi was born in Medina on 13 October 1958 to a well-connected family. Their roots were Turkish and their name means 'spice maker'. His grandfather Mohammed Khaled Khashoggi had moved from the city of Kayseri, in Anatolia, to the Hejaz region of the Arabian peninsula when both were still under Ottoman rule. He became personal physician to King Ibn Saud the founder of Saudi Arabia, a status that allowed his family to achieve prominence. Mohammed was father of late billionaire arms dealer Adnan Khashoggi, the middleman in the Iran-Contra scandal in the 1980s. Adnan was also once neighbour of Donald Trump and sold him a $200-million yacht. Khashoggi's aunt was Samira, who married Mohamed al-Fayed, the former Egyptian owner of Harrods who had been refused a UK passport on account of not being 'a fit and proper person'.

After receiving his primary and secondary

education in Medina, Jamal Khashoggi went to the US to study business administration, at Indiana State University, graduating with a bachelor's degree in 1982. His first wife was Rawia al-Tunisi. They had two sons, Salah and Abdullah, and two daughters, Noha and Razan. They were all educated in America and three of them took US citizenship. At the time, of his assassination Khashoggi's sons were banned from leaving Saudi Arabia.

After graduating, Khashoggi returned to Saudi Arabia where his first job was as the manager of a group of bookshops. By the mid-1980s, however, he was writing for English-language newspapers such as the *Saudi Gazette* and *Arab News*. From 1991 to 1999, he worked as a foreign correspondent in such countries as Afghanistan, Algeria, Kuwait, Sudan, and in the Middle East, reporting on the First Gulf War. To the outside world became well-known for his interviews with Osama bin Laden, who had been a prominent member of the mujahideen resistance against Soviet-Russia's push in Afghanistan, much of it funded by the Saudis and Americans – spear-headed by the Bush family – then perturbed by the spread of Communism. (It was only after the Russian withdrawal from Afghanistan that bin Laden turned on his American backers through forming al-Qaeda.)

It was as foreign correspondent that Khashoggi had become a trusted asset for Saudi intelligence and later a confidant of powerful Saudi royals such as long-standing intelligence chief Prince Turki al-Faisal. During his time in Afghanistan, Khashoggi came to know Osama bin Laden well, interviewing him at his hideout in the Tora Bora mountains, then later in Sudan. He was one of the few links (if not the only one) to bin Laden that the Saudi and US intelligence services had until then.

According to fellow *Washington Post* columnist David Ignatius, 'Khashoggi couldn't have travelled with the mujahideen that way without tacit support from Saudi intelligence, which was co-ordinating aid to the fighters as part of its co-operation with the CIA against the Soviet Union in Afghanistan.' At the time Khashoggi criticised Prince Salman, MBS's father, then head of the Saudi committee for support to the Afghan mujahideen, for funding Salafist extremist groups that were undermining the efforts of the other guerillas.

Even before his friendship with bin Laden, Khashoggi had had a personal interest in political Islam. After the Iranian revolution in 1979 and the rise to power of Ayatollah Khomeini, he began attending Islamic conferences and meetings in Indiana and became very religious. Khashoggi admitted that as a young man he had joined the Muslim Brotherhood, the reformist movement begun in Egypt in the 1920s and which was then supported by Saudi Arabia. He since renounced it and many of his writings revealed sympathy for a more secular and religiously pluralist kingdom. Given Saudi Arabia's strict adherence to Wahhabism, with which Khashoggi had no problem as such, he was not much of a political dissident (if he ever was one).

Khashoggi had first met bin Laden, who was Saudi by birth, in Jeddah in the early 1980s. They were the same age.

'Osama was just like many of us who became part of the Brotherhood movement in Saudi Arabia,' Khashoggi said. 'The only difference that set him apart from others, and me, he was more religious. More religious, more literal, more fundamentalist. For example, he would not listen to music. He would not shake hands with a woman. He would not smoke. He would not watch television, unless it was news. He wouldn't play cards. He would not put a picture on his wall. But more than that, there was also a harsh or radical side in his life. I'm sure you have some people like that in your culture. For example, even though he comes from a rich family, he lives in a very simple house.'

In Afghanistan he got to know bin Laden better. He was impressed with his enthusiasm and devotion. In 1987, this gave him a scoop.

'I interviewed Osama – a gentle, enthusiastic young man of few words who didn't raise his voice while talking,' he said. They discussed the condition of the mujahideen and what bin Laden was doing to help them. 'I did not know him thoroughly enough to judge him or expect any other thing from him. His behaviour at that time left no impression that he would become what he has become.'

Al-Qaeda was founded in 1988 as the Soviets were withdrawing from Afghanistan. Bin Laden talked of spreading jihad through central Asia. There was no talk of attacking the United States or Europe. Bin Laden and Khashoggi had met for the last time in the Sudan in 1995.

'Osama was almost about to change his mind and reconcile and come back to Saudi Arabia,' he said. 'It was a lost opportunity.'

Although Khashoggi was asked to try to persuade bin Laden to renounce violence and failed, he retained the ear of powerful members of the ruling house. Khashoggi was surprised when bin Laden announced he was declaring war on America in 1997 and shocked by the attacks on 9/11. He gave up the idea of creating an Islamic state in Saudi Arabia. 'I think we must find a way where we can accommodate secularism and Islam, something like what they have in Turkey,' he said.

When bin Laden was killed in 2011, Khashoggi wrote on Twitter: 'I collapsed crying a while ago, heartbroken for you Abu Abdullah [bin Laden's nickname]. You were beautiful and brave in those beautiful days in Afghanistan, before you surrendered to hatred and passion.'

The rewards for loyalty to the Saudi royal family

during the turbulence in Afghanistan were great. In 1991, Khashoggi had become editor of al-*Madina*, one of Jeddah's oldest newspapers, and in 1999, Khashoggi rose further to become the deputy editor-in-chief on *Arab News*, the biggest English language daily in the kingdom, and a key interlocutor for western journalists with the Saudi royal family, whose formal apparatus was often impenetrable to the outside world. He was also a valuable source for foreign journalists trying to understand the rise of Islamism.

Four years later he became the editor-in-chief of the Saudi Arabian daily al-*Watan*. But here he fell foul of Saudi Arabia's deeply conservative religious sectarianism. After less than two months, he was dismissed by the Saudi Arabian Ministry of Information because he had allowed a columnist to question the fourteen-century Islamic scholar Ibn Taymiyyah, who was the founding father of Wahhabism, the ultra-conservative form of Sunni Islam which is the state religion of Saudi Arabia. Such rebuffs from religious conservatives were to mark the remainder of his career.

He went into voluntary exile in London by becoming media adviser to the urbane Prince Turki al-Faisal, grandson of Saudi Arabia's founder, now ambassador in London after having been the head of the Saudi intelligence from 1977 to 2001 during the Soviet-Afghanistan crisis. Khashoggi was permitted in 2007 to return to al-*Watan* as editor but was dismissed a second time three years later, this time for himself criticising the kingdom's harsh Islamic rules.

'The clergy. They didn't like me,' he said. 'They didn't like the way I ran the paper. Totally lobbied against me and they got me out. I miss journalism and I think it's a very interesting time in my country. I see change, and I would like to be part of that change.'

Khashoggi continued to contribute regularly to the media, including foreign broadcasters, building up his nearly two million followers on Twitter. In 2015 he agreed to become editor-in-chief of a new news channel based in Bahrain, Al-Arab. Backed by Saudi Arabian billionaire Prince Alwaleed bin Talal and partnered with US financial news channel Bloomberg Television, it was meant to be a rival to al-Jazeera, which is supported by Qatar. However, it was closed down by the Bahraini government on its first day after interviewing a member of the opposition. Alwaleed bin Talal was detained by MBS during his shakedown in 2017.

He continued working as a political commentator for Saudi Arabian and international channels, including MBC, BBC, al-Jazeera, and Dubai TV. Between June 2012 and September 2016, his opinion columns were regularly broadcast by the Saudi-owned pan-Arab news channel al-*Arabiya*. However, he was critical of the conduct of the war in Yemen and found himself at odds with Crown Prince Mohammed bin Salman, particularly over his crackdown on dissent. But he was only barred by the Saudi authorities from publishing or appearing on television when he criticised U.S. president-elect Donald Trump during the think-tank event in Washington, DC.

He published three books, including in 2016 a study of the Arab Spring. In June 2017, after a series of arrests, Khashoggi fled Saudi Arabia with only two suitcases and found refuge in the US where he wrote a monthly column for the *Washington Post* and was heralded as the most famous political pundit in the Arab world.

In his column, he continued his worrying criticism of President Trump, as well as repressive Arab regimes and particularly MBS, who was concerned by the fact that Khashoggi knew intimately the inner workings and political alignments of the secretive Saudi royal family. That rare understanding alone was of a strategic importance to the kingdom and MBS's adversaries.

The fact that he was associated with positions ideologically close to the Muslim Brotherhood, which the Crown Prince hated with a passion, made things worse. Khashoggi rejected the term dissident, but his decision to write for the *Washington Post* must have also been considered an insult. The fact that the paper began translating his pieces into Arabic would have no doubt riled him.

MBS was also concerned about the pro-Qatari line Khashoggi had been taking in recent columns in the *Washington Post* and he was to have been a guest speaker at the Gulf International Form's inaugural conference at the National Press Club in Washington, DC, on 16 October, which was funded by the Qataris.

The Crown Prince made a traditional tribal offer of reconciliation – offering him a place as an adviser if he returned to the kingdom. Khashoggi had declined because of moral and religious principles, and, perhaps more to the point, valuing his own safety. He told the BBC that he was 'worried for my country, my children and grandchildren – one-man rule is always bad, in any country'.

He was also in danger because he had helped established a new political party in the US called Democracy for the Arab World Now, which would support Islamist gains in democratic elections throughout the region. He was also planning a campaign and a 'cyberwar' against the Saudi regime.

Khashoggi had been married and divorced three times. At the time of his death, he had just got engaged. His fiancée was thirty-six-year-old Hatice Cengiz, a PhD student at university in Istanbul. The two of them had met at a conference in May, where he gave a speech. She knew who he was and followed his work. Afterwards she asked him a question and the two of them soon got talking. A relationship developed and they soon got engaged, planning to marry on his sixtieth birthday. Her father opposed the match as Khashoggi was fifty-nine. He thought the age gap was too great, but eventually relented. Ms Cengiz said her fiancé had had to choose between returning to Saudi Arabia or visiting one of the consulates for the necessary papers after they decided to marry.

'When we first went on 28 September, Jamal was worried that something could go wrong. But when he entered the consulate on 28 September, everything went OK and the atmosphere was comfortable,' she said. There were no problems, even though they knew who he was. They had been lulled into a false sense of security.

The following day, Khashoggi attended a conference in London where he criticised Saudi Arabia. At the event, he told BBC *Newshour*: 'An event like that would be difficult to hold today in the Arab world because we are retreating from freedom in most of the Arab countries. Most of the Arab world is currently collapsing, for example in Libya, Syria and Yemen and has no interest in discussing Palestine because they have miseries of their own. Then in countries like Saudi Arabia, my country, or in Egypt, they have no interest in those kinds of issues that motivate and rally the people because they want to subdue them instead.'

That evening he had dinner with Daud Abdullah, a former editor and translator at the Abul Qasim Publishing House in Jeddah, and other colleagues and guests who attended the conference in a Turkish restaurant in Bloomsbury. Two days later, he flew back to Istanbul.

4
Dead End

ൟ

Before Jamal Khashoggi returned to the consulate in Istanbul on 2 October, US intelligence intercepted communications of Saudi officials discussing a plan to capture him. This intelligence had been disseminated throughout the U.S. government and was contained in reports that are routinely available to people working on U.S. policy toward Saudi Arabia. It was not clear whether the Saudis intended to arrest, or to kidnap, torture and interrogate Khashoggi, or to kill him. Khashoggi was a US resident and, under internal government order ICD19-'Duty to Warn', US intelligence services were under a duty to warn him of potential kidnapping or murder.

Nonetheless, the decision was taken not to warn Khashoggi of the Saudi plans.

Not that Khashoggi himself trusted the Saudi government. According to his friend and fellow member of the Turkish Arab Media Association Turan Kişlakçi, Khashoggi was nervous about returning to the consulate. He left his laptop, mobile phone and other valuables with his fiancée before he went in.

'He told her if he didn't show up after a few hours, call the Turkish Arab Media Centre and Turkish authorities,' said Kişlakçi the following day, 3 October. 'We believe he's still inside. There was no sign that he was taken out in a black car or something. Maybe they are interrogating him.'

But Khashoggi had also told Kişlakçi that he had no fear: 'I'm not afraid, because there is no official investigation against me. On the contrary, recently, [Crown Prince] Mohammed bin Salman asked me to be his adviser, and I refused, saying this is against my country and region's interests.... The most they can do is interrogate me. And I can give them answers, I have nothing to hide.' In fact, on 3 October, asked by Bloomberg 'Is he facing any charges in Saudi Arabia?', MBS was evasive. Pressed by Bloomberg, 'So he might be facing charges in Saudi Arabia?', MBS ignored the question and repeated what he had said before, 'If he's in Saudi Arabia I would know that'.

According to Kişlakçi: 'His fiancée's father pressured him to get the relevant documents to initiate the official marriage process in Turkey. His trusted Saudi friends in the US gave him assurance. He was confident in what he was doing.'

Doubtless he felt that, in particular, that his growing closeness to President Erdoğan worked in his favour. Over breakfast that morning, he told Hatice he thought it unlikely that Saudi officials would risk angering Turkey by detaining him. In fact, it was like a red flag to a bull.

'Jamal said to me: they can't do something like that in Turkey,' she said. But at the same time he was anxious, even though he was not aware of any criminal charges against him.

'He didn't want to go,' she said. 'He was nervous that something could happen.'

They agreed that Ms Cengiz should skip classes that day to accompany him. While he went into the consulate, she waited outside a nearby supermarket.

'I waited a really long time,' she said. 'I thought they must be sorting the papers. At 3.30pm the staff went home. I realised that something strange had happened.'

Ms Cengiz went the consulate to find out where her fiancé was. She said a man came to the entrance who told her that there was no one inside, so she called Yasin Aktay, a Turkish journalist who was a close friend of Khashoggi's and an adviser to Turkey's President Recep Tayyip Erdoğan. She also informed the police. Meanwhile, she hung on outside the consulate, hoping against hope, for eleven hours.

The day after Khashoggi visited the consulate, Al-Jazeera, the TV station based in Qatar and a Saudi bane, was reporting that he had been abducted. Some seventy thousand tweets were discussing his disappearance – though many said they doubted Saudi involvement, alleging a conspiracy between Turkey and the Muslim Brotherhood – deemed a terrorist organisation in Saudi Arabia – to defame the kingdom.

Others, though, were already pointing the finger at MBS. One commentator wrote: 'If news of abducting Jamal Khashoggi is true, it will be one of the biggest follies of Mohammed bin Salman. The man has an international standing and reputation. It will not go unnoticed.'

Another, quoting a source who claimed to be close to the Royal Court, said that Khashoggi had indeed been abducted and was smuggled into Saudi Arabia arriving there in the early hours.

'If it is true, it is would be difficult to imagine Turkey standing idly by while Mohammed bin Salman is playing with its sovereignty before the world,' the tweet thundered.

Ms Cenzig was now beside herself with worry.

'I don't know what has happened to him,' she said. 'I can't even guess how such a thing can happen to him. There is no law or lawsuit against him. He is not a suspect, he has not been convicted. There is nothing against him. He is just a man whose country doesn't like his writings or his opinions.'

The Turkish government still had no idea what had happened with Khashoggi either. A Turkish security official was quoted saying they were in discussion with the Saudis and believed that Khashoggi was still being held in the consulate.

Turkey's misunderstanding of what had happened in the consulate was confirmed by President Erdoğan himself. 'According to the information that we have, this Saudi citizen is still in the Saudi Arabian consulate in Istanbul,' said Ibrahim Kalin, Turkey's presidential spokesperson.

'We don't have any information to the contrary. We

continue to follow this issue closely.'

However, echoing MBS's statement to Bloomberg on 3 October, Saudi authorities issued a statement flatly denying he was being detained, and claiming that Khashoggi 'visited the consulate and exited shortly thereafter'.

That very week, economist Essam al-Zamil, a friend of Khashoggi's and critic of the Crown Prince's selling part of Aramco, was charged with joining the Muslim Brotherhood, providing in information to foreign diplomats and inciting protests. Meanwhile the *Washington Post* issued a statement concerning the fate of its columnist.

'We have been unable to reach Jamal today and are very concerned about where he may be,' said Eli Lopez, the newspaper's international opinions editor. 'It would be unfair and outrageous if he has been detained for his work as a journalist and commentator.'

Calls and emails to Saudi missions in London, Washington, and Istanbul yielded no further information about Khashoggi. The Turkish newspaper and government-mouthpiece *Milliyet* was reporting on 3 October what Erdoğan's spokesperson had said: 'The Saudi journalist could not leave the consulate building.'

In the dark, the Turkish government applied diplomatic pressure. The Saudi ambassador in Ankara was summoned to the Turkish Foreign Ministry to clear up the matter. He told the Turkish deputy foreign minister that he had no information about the missing journalist.

'We are investigating,' he said. 'I will convey any information we get.' It was the diplomatic equivalent of saying 'don't hold your breath on our account.'

The Saudis used the situation to cause further confusion with some Saudi officials saying that Khashoggi never entered the consulate and others saying he entered and then left. In effect, they were implying that Ms Cenzig, who had dropped him off at the embassy, was a liar.

The police were also at work on the case. 'The missing persons department has launched works upon the application of Jamal Khashoggi's family,' reported the nationalist opposition newspaper *Sözcü*. 'Police teams have launched a broad investigation to find Khashoggi, primarily analysing city surveillance footage.'

The story from Saudi Arabia itself was different, with the state-run Saudi Press Agency reporting on 4 October, the now official version: 'The consulate has confirmed that it is co-ordinating with the brotherly local Turkish authorities in the follow-up procedures to reveal the circumstances surrounding the disappearance of citizen Jamal Khashoggi after having left the consulate building.'

The ostensible promise of sweeping access to the Saudi consulate in Istanbul was sanctioned by Riyadh. In the wide-ranging Bloomberg interview on many topics on the night of 3 October MBS had already given his personal promise to allow the same thing. Of Khashoggi, whom he called 'Jamal' to indicate his friendship and personal investment in the matter, MBS said, 'Yes, he's not inside.' This was, by this time, 100 per cent true and there was no risk when he said the 'premises are sovereign territory' and he would 'allow [the Turkish government] to enter and search and do whatever they want to do.'

Nonetheless, social media users were not convinced and continued to say that Khashoggi was being held at the Saudi consulate. Others speculated he had been smuggled back into Saudi Arabia. Khashoggi's personal website bore a banner headline saying: 'Jamal has been arrested at the Saudi Consulate in Istanbul!' Again the Saudi Arabian authorities issued a statement denying he was being detained, safe in the knowledge that this was true. Supporters of MBS continued arguing that the whole story had been made up to smear the kingdom.

Turkey was still entirely in the dark and a spokesman for Turkey's President Erdoğan said: 'According to information we have, this individual who is a Saudi national is still at the Istanbul consulate of Saudi Arabia.' Turkey's government was in the dark what had happened to Khashoggi inside the consulate. It only knew that he had gone in and had not left the building. It had, at this point, no more information than what his fiancée and media friends had.

And his fiancée was adamant, saying: 'We want to know his whereabouts. Where is Jamal? We want him to come out of the consulate safe and sound.'

She subscribed to the theory that he had been kidnapped. 'If that's not what happened, where is Jamal?' she asked. 'Right now we have no information. As a missing person, he is in danger.'

She said that the Turkish authorities were working hard to locate her fiancé and wanted to believe that he had not been smuggled out of the country.

'I want to be positive, I want to be hopeful,' she said. 'I hope that Jamal is in Istanbul.'

Karen Attiah, Khashoggi's editor at the *Washington Post*, said the newspaper had still not been able to reach him.

'We have inquired about Jamal's whereabouts, and expressed our deep concern, to both Turkish and Saudi officials,' she said.

On Friday 5 October, the *Post* printed left his column blank to show solidarity with their missing columnist. It bore Khashoggi's byline and photograph, and was headlined: 'A missing voice.'

A note from the editor read: 'Jamal Khashoggi is a Saudi journalist and author, and a columnist for *Washington Post* Global Opinions. Khashoggi's words should appear in the space above, but he has not been heard from since he entered a Saudi consulate in Istanbul for a routine consular matter on Tuesday afternoon.'

Clutching at straws given Turkey's and Saudi-Arabia's antipathy to investigative journalism, the *Post* called on the Crown Prince to 'do everything in his power to ensure that Mr Khashoggi is free and able to continue his work'.

In an editorial, the newspaper said: 'Mr Khashoggi is not just any commentator. Over a long career, he has had close contact with Saudi royalty and knows more than most about how they think and function. His criticism, voiced over the past year, most surely rankles Mohammed bin Salman, who was elevated to crown prince last year and has carried out a wide-ranging campaign to silence dissent while trying to modernize the kingdom. Among those in his prisons for political speech are clerics, bloggers, journalists and activists. He imprisoned women who agitated for the right to drive, a right that was granted even as they were punished.'

The *Post*'s editorial board also made a direct appeal to MBS: 'The Crown Prince has been all over the United States preaching his vision of a more modern Saudi society, breaking out of the stale old religious codes and practices, opening up to foreign entertainment and investment. If he is truly committed to this, he will welcome constructive criticism from patriots such as Mr Khashoggi.'

Journalists from the Turkish Arab Media Association meanwhile staged a protest outside the Saudi consulate in Istanbul.

'We demand the immediate release of Jamal Khashoggi, who we think is being 'hosted' at the consulate building in Istanbul, or the revealing of his whereabouts,' said Turan Kişlakçi, the association's president. 'If they do not release him we will stand here for weeks and months. We will stage the same demonstrations of solidarity not just here but everywhere in the world.'

The New York-based group Human Rights Watch took a keen interest. Middle East director Sarah Leah Whitson said: 'If Saudi authorities surreptitiously detained Khashoggi it would be yet another escalation of Crown Prince Mohammed bin Salman's reign of repression against peaceful dissidents and critics. The burden of proof is on Saudi Arabia to produce evidence for its claim that Khashoggi left the consulate alone, and that Saudi agents have not detained him.'

MBS seemed to hold all the cards. Without further facts the storm would soon die out.

5

Thunderbolt

৯

In the 3 October Wednesday night interview with Bloomberg, Crown Prince Mohammed bin Salman had volunteered extremely definitive information on Khashoggi's whereabouts. The detail was such that, if untrue, his words would come straight back to haunt him.

'If he's in Saudi Arabia, I would know that,' MBS had answered confidently.

Given his insistence, there is no reason to assume that the hit squad had repatriated Khashoggi's remains to Saudi Arabia. No one on the Saudi side could care less where the 'traitor' would be disposed of.

Contradicting the words of Khashoggi's fiancée who had been waiting outside the consulate's front door, MBS also volunteered, 'My understanding is he entered and he got out after a few minutes or one hour'.

But with the far easier question – as with the equally easy Bloomberg question whether there were any charges against Khashoggi's – MBS's claimed to be unsure and added words to fuel the uncertainty. 'I'm not sure. We are investigating this through the foreign ministry to see exactly what happened at that time.'

Amiably, he had also directed subtle blame regarding the fate of his 'friend' Jamal at his totalitarian neighbour President Erdoğan. 'We hear the rumours about what happened,' said MBS. 'He's a Saudi citizen and we are very keen to know what happened to him. And we will continue our dialogue with the Turkish government to see what happened to Jamal there.'

The Crown Prince had elegantly used the rest of the Bloomberg interview both to brandish his profile as a new broom and as a conservative while dispatching any criticism of him personally as a consequence of the machinations of the kingdom's enemies.

'I didn't call myself a reformer of Saudi Arabia,' he said. 'I am the Crown Prince of Saudi Arabia and I am trying to do the best that I can do through my position.'

He addressed the arrest of women's rights activists in his kingdom and accused them of espionage. It was the same blame-the-enemy strategy that his supporters on social media used.

'They have connections with agencies of other countries,' he said, naming Iran and Qatar. 'They have a network, connection with government people, leaking information for the sake these other governments.'

The activists, who had been calling for women's right to drive, had not been formally charged and were denied contact with their families since they were arrested five months earlier.

Interestingly he also addressed Donald Trump,

casting light on the reasons why Khashoggi had been muzzled two days after Trump had won the election. On exactly the same day Khashoggi had been assassinated, the US president had in an extraordinary statement said at a political rally in Mississipi: 'We protect Saudi Arabia. Would you say they're rich? And I love the King, King Salman. But I said "King – we're protecting you – you might not be there for two weeks without us – you have to pay for your military".' Donald Trump's statement was so unusual that it became instant global news, though only the intelligence services in the know were aware how timely the seemingly random demand for money was.

MBS was adamant that the Saudi royal family were no puppets who were in power merely hiding behind the skirts of the US akin to the Shah of Persia. He smoothly brushed off Trump's comment.

'We believe that all the armaments we have from the United States of America are paid for, it's not free armament,' said MBS, focusing on Trump's clumsy suggestion that the US paid the Saudi military. 'So ever since the relationship started between Saudi Arabia and the United States of America, we've bought everything with money.'

Money was one thing Saudi Arabia had plenty of. Warmly MBS went on to signal his delight with fellow billionaire Donald Trump, who had registered eight companies in the Saudi beach resort Jeddah shortly after launching his presidential campaign in order to expand his business interests. Trump already had a hotel bearing his name in neighbouring UAE, MBS closest regional ally.

'I love working with him,' MBS gushed. 'You know, you have to accept that any friend will say good things and bad things. If you look at the picture overall, you have 99 per cent of good things and one bad issue.'

Then, on Saturday 6 October, everything changed.

Suddenly real information it had not previously possessed had come into the hands of the Turkish government.

A leak to a respected US-based academic summarised what Turkey knew from its own surveillance up to now.

Whatever had happened to Jamal Khashoggi, it was not good – 'and by not good, I mean terrible,' Washington-based Turkish scholar Selim Sazak said that a senior Turkish official had leaked to him.

'They don't know that Jamal Khashoggi was murdered,' Sazak said. 'They know that he came in, didn't come out. They saw unusual personnel activity, including uncredentialled personnel, coming to the embassy almost immediately after Jamal Khashoggi's first visit so they think they were dispatched from Riyadh, and they speak of an unknown staffer, acting like he was moving out the embassy, packing stuff into his trunk, and leaving at the end of business the day Jamal Khashoggi disappeared. So they add up the pieces to infer that

Jamal Khashoggi was incapacitated and spirited away.'

But 6 October was the day on which all of a sudden a torrent of 20/20 factual information on the fateful last hours of Khashoggi after he entered the consulate at 1:14pm on 2 October was to be leaked.

Given its uninformed statements over the previous days, where did the Turkish government get all this new eye-watering detail from on what had happened inside the consulate? If MIT, the Turkish intelligence service, already knew what had really happened to Khashoggi President Erdoğan would not seem so clueless with hindsight. Turkey had been blamed for Khashoggi's disappearance by MBS. Erdoğan had been played.

The detailed information certainly did not come to Turkey from the Americans. The US government had sailed into risky territory by not warning Khashoggi of the widely circulated intel that Saudi Arabia was about to move against him. That decision to keep lethal information from a US resident would look very suspiciously like tit for tat if it was widely known that on the very same day of Khashoggi's assassination Trump had started to shake down the kingdom for US protection money. In the light of murder, even the fact that Khashoggi had been told in Washington to go to Istanbul to complete marriage formalities, would look suspiciously as if the US had known enough to warn Saudi Arabia not to try and capture Khashoggi anywhere on US soil. The US government had everything to gain from letting sleeping dogs lie.

Under oath, government officials would defend themselves with the paper-thin argument that it wasn't clear whether Khashoggi would be lawfully arrested or illegally detained or killed.

The argument itself was very plausible in the case of a disappearance. In case of a lawful arrest, there was in any case no duty on the US intelligence services to pre-warn a US resident. But in the case of an assassination, the same argument would look like incompetence at best and tacit cooperation in the killing of a US journalist by the US government at the worst.

The US knew that something was afoot and undoubtedly knew exactly, like the Russians, what took place on 2 October. But there was no upside in embarrassing MBS, an otherwise enthusiastic ally of their commander in chief, Donald Trump, who himself had his business future after his presidency to consider.

There was also another fact. Although Erdoğan was an autocrat after Trump's heart, he had seriously irked Trump by not releasing Andrew Brunson, the US pastor Turkey held captive since the putsch against Erdoğan in the summer of 2016. Following Trump's angry tweets against Turkey on the subject of Brunson, there was little love lost in Washington for the truculent Erdoğan.

Who, then, benefited from leaking detailed information about the murder, and pulling the rug from underneath the 'disappearance' story? Karl Marx used to ask the question, 'who benefits?', to reconstruct who was behind events.

One has to look no further than the words of Vladimir Putin at the Valdai Discussion conference of 18 October in the Black-sea beach resort Sochi to see who benefitted most from ending the disappearance speculation by leaking the blow-by-blow detail of Khashoggi's killing.

Echoing Donald Trump's official response, on that day Putin declined action against Saudi Arabia on account of the Khashoggi affair. He whole-heartedly agreed that more facts were needed about Saudi governmental involvement before taking measures against the kingdom as a whole. 'We first need to wait for the results of the investigation' who is behind the assassination, Putin said. 'How can we, as Russia, start to harm our relationship with Saudi Arabia without knowing what really happened?'

Then followed the rub. Gleefully, Putin drew a comparison between Khashoggi and the poisoning in Salisbury with *novichok*, the state of the art Russian nerve agent, of Sergei Skripal, his daughter, Det. Sgt Nick Bailey, Charley Rowley, as well as the agonising death of Dawn Sturgess a little over two months earlier in Britain.

Complaining bitterly about US and European sanctions against Russia over the *novichok* attack in Salisbury he pointed out 'There's no proof in regards to Russia, but steps are taken.' The facts in Khashoggi's case were no different, he claimed. 'Here, people say that a murder happened in Istanbul, but no steps are taken [against Saudi Arabia]. People need to figure out a single approach to these kinds of problems.' The *novichok* furore was, in other words, incredibly unfair on Russia.

In a further dig at the US, Putin also leaked information from Russian intelligence files when he said, that 'the US bears a certain responsibility'. Certainly Trump's public criticism and demand for more Saudi money couldn't have been better timed than on the day Khashoggi entered the Istanbul consulate never to return. Putin added as an aside, 'we can see that complicated processes are also taking place within the US elites. I hope America will not go as far as Saudi Arabia did.' Keen to taunt the US, Putin had ended up seemingly cryptically to confirm that Russian intelligence knew exactly what Saudi Arabia had done, and more.

Other countries without a free media formed a chorus line behind Putin. A Chinese media outlet helpfully connected the dots made by him. Eager to make clear that citizens' rights were no more than a cudgel for the West to bully other countries with, the Chinese outlet commented sourly that it 'shows that there are double, even multiple standards for the West's human rights diplomacy'.

Having excellent relations with President Erdoğan,

and detailed knowledge of anything that goes on in Turkey and Istanbul in particular, is crucially important to Russia – much more so than for the US with whom Turkey is a NATO ally. Russia's one and only warm-water shipping and naval route runs from the Black Sea through the Bosphorus to the Mediterranean. This route is so important that when the EU looked close to wooing Ukraine into its fold, Vladimir Putin didn't think twice about occupying the Crimea and its Black-Sea ports for both commercial and military reasons.

Putin, like the US, had the intelligence about Khashoggi's fate. But unlike the US it had an excellent reason for sharing it with Turkey .

On 6 October, the Turkish police thus suddenly changed tack. They were now claiming that Khashoggi wasn't missing but had been murdered in the Saudi consulate.

'The initial assessment of the Turkish police is that Mr Khashoggi has been killed at the consulate of Saudi Arabia in Istanbul,' two Turkish officials said off the record. 'We believe that the murder was premeditated and the body was subsequently moved out of the consulate.'

Suddenly the fact that Turkey thought (and therefore had miraculously obtained precise information) that Khashoggi's fate was premeditated murder hit the international media like a thunderbolt. In countries with a free press it was stop-the-press news because they were appalled. In the ones without, it was front-page news because it was an excellent object lesson for those with ideas.

The official leaks gained momentum.

Yasi Aktay, advisor to President Erdoğan, thundered on CNN to the Saudis: 'There is concrete information; it will not remain an unsolved case. If they consider Turkey to be as it was in the 1990s, they are mistaken.'

He said it was clear that a team of fifteen Saudis who had arrived on 2 October had been sent there to kill him, Kişlakçi said. The government in Riyadh knew that he would be there then as he had been told to return the consulate on Tuesday when he had visited on the 28th.

Khashoggi's media friend Kişlakçi had been given some more colour by officials: 'They followed the cars, and they know what happened. We have all the details, and he was killed.'

Ms Cengiz was aghast and found the new twist to the story hard to believe. She tweeted: 'Jamal was not killed and I cannot believe he was killed!' She later added that she was waiting for official confirmation from the Turkish government of the leaks by its officials.

Others still agreed with her. 'If Saudi authorities surreptitiously detained Khashoggi it would be yet another escalation of Crown Prince Mohammed bin Salman's reign of repression against peaceful dissidents and critics,' said Sarah Leah Whitson, Middle East director of Human Rights Watch. 'The burden of proof is on Saudi Arabia to produce evidence for its claim that Khashoggi left the consulate alone, and that Saudi agents have not detained him.'

The *Washington Post* gave the report credence though. 'If the reports of Jamal's murder are true, it is a monstrous and unfathomable act,' said Fred Hiatt, the *Washington Post*'s editorial page editor. 'Jamal was – or, as we hope, is – a committed, courageous journalist. He writes out of a sense of love for his country and deep faith in human dignity and freedom.'

Over the course of the day, Saudi Arabia was all of a sudden on the backfoot. Officials continued to claim that Khashoggi entered the consulate but left shortly afterwards. But they released no CCTV footage to back up the claim – for the obvious reason that there was none. The Saudis still hoped that there was no real proof against their version of events.

President Erdoğan himself also still hedged his bets, although he now knew what had happened to his 'friend': 'I hope we will not be faced with a situation that we do not want,' he said, describing the veteran commentator as 'a friend' and 'a journalist I have known for a long time' – a rather dubious epithet coming from the president, but a word that was catnip to the Western media. Behind the scenes, Erdoğan was now hoping to leverage a deal based on the intelligence that had suddenly come into his possession.

His advisor Yasin Aktay signalled what was going to be Turkey's new line by going on the record with the new line: 'My sense is that he has been killed. The Saudis are saying we can come investigate, but they have of course disposed of the body.'

Leaks to Khashoggi's friend Turan Kişlakçi drove the point home further what Turkey's new intelligence entailed.

'It is certain that he was killed,' he said, claiming that authorities had evidence (that is to had leaked to him) that he had been killed in a 'barbaric' way.

The Turkish authorities had not yet produced any proof to support claims that Khashoggi had been murdered, saying only in measured words that details would be made public in the days ahead. Nor had President Erdoğan publicly challenged Riyadh because officials were trying to keep the diplomatic fallout 'under control' – a polite way of saying that he was offering the Saudis a horse trade to keep his intel under lock and key.

Meanwhile prosecutors were investigating and the police had helpfully made the connection between Khashoggi's disappearance and the fifteen Saudis who had flown into Istanbul that day and paid a flying visit to the consulate.

'Based on their initial findings, the police believe that the journalist was killed by a team especially sent to Istanbul and who left the same day,' an official leaked.

Ömer Çelik, a spokesman for the ruling Justice and Development (AK) Party, snapped further at the heels of Saudi Arabia: 'A journalist disappearing like this in a secure country like the Republic of Turkey is something that will be followed up with sensitivity.'

MBS was not in the mood for a horse trade and publicly protested the accusations resulting from the Turkish leaks, insisting that Khashoggi had left the consulate after his appointment and that claims of his murder were 'baseless'.

Although the Turkish officials had not yet been given the promised access to investigate the consulate forensically (because 'we have nothing to hide' in MBS's words), the Saudi consul general in Istanbul, Mohammed al-Otaibi, had invited Reuters on a tour of the six-storey premises on 6 October.

'We are worried about him,' Mohammed al-Otaibi said on camera. But giving away the lie that was on his mind, he looked like a gruesome Mr Bean while opening cupboards, filing cabinets and wooden panels covering air conditioning units of his consulate on TV in an attempt to show that there was no sign of Khashoggi there. 'But look, he is not here', he tried to reassure the journalists.

While the consulate was equipped with security cameras, Mr al-Otaibi said that they could not provide images of the Khashoggi leaving. But the suggestion that he had been abducted in the building was 'disgusting' and based on 'rumours that have no proof'. A review of CCTV footage of the outside of the building by Turkish authorities, however, had already concluded that he had not left.

The matter could easily be resolved. Fred Hiatt at the *Post* said: 'If the story that was told about the murder is true, the Turks must have information and videotape and other documents to back it up. If the story the Saudis are telling, that he just walked out... after half an hour, if that's true, they ought to have facts and documents and evidence and tapes to back that up.'

It was a fair point, but whether Turkey would do so was another.

With the Turkish economy wilting the increasingly strained relations with the US and Donald Trump in particular weren't helping. The tapes were a golden opportunity for Erdoğan to pivot things around with some effective arm-twisting behind the scenes.

6

Pastor Brunson

～

The fate of pastor Andrew Brunson was like a buoy floating on the surface, tethered to discussions between the autocrats involved. The Turkish economy, once seemingly unstoppable, was sagging and Erdoğan needed to nurture a flow of US money (or Saudi money or Russian money, preferably all three to remain independent). The Khashoggi-assassination had finally landed Turkey the upper hand in this endeavour.

For the US, the incarceration of pastor Brunson had been one of the reasons they had put their NATO ally in the diplomatic deep freeze. Brunson's incarceration had been a November 2016-election rallying cry for Trump's evangelical voters for whom Mike Pence was the Brunson-*cause célèbre*'s poster child. Despite persistent pressure from the US, where the Christian conservative lobby relentlessly agitated for his release, and where Trump regularly tweeted about this 'great Christian' whose release was a 2016 election promise, Erdoğan stubbornly refused to release the pastor. This was in itself curious as Brunson had had a flock of no more than 24 congregants. But for Turkey, Brunson was symbolically connected with the man whom Erdoğan blamed for the 15 July 2016 coup against him. This man, Fethullah Gülen, lived in longstanding exile in

Saylorsburg, Pennsylvania, protected by the US from extradition.

'Working very hard on Pastor Brunson!' Trump excitedly tweeted on the Friday, 3 days after Khashoggi's assassination.

Indeed, all of a sudden, Turkey decided to drop its intransigence and to release Brunson within a week, leading to a triumphant photo opportunity for Trump on 13 October in the White House with the now free Brunson tearfully praying for Trump to have 'super-natural wisdom' – a fervent wish that made sense given Donald Trump's disinterest in Christian or any other doctrine. (Other collateral damage of the 2016 coup, such as a number of US consulate workers and the holidaying NASA scientist Serkan Golge, had no such publicity value and these people were not so lucky. They remained locked up – in the case of Golge in solitary confinement.) Another, four weeks later, more evidence of the sudden thaw in the relations would emerge when both Turkey and the US shortly after one another started 'unilaterally' to roll back sanctions against black-listed government officials.

It is clear what Turkey had to gain, and would promise – no US embarrassment – but what exactly Turkey had on the US that brought its government to the negotiation table is a lot less clear.

However, with a script agreed between the US and Turkey and tokens of goodwill accepted and exchanged, Turkey was now free to pursue Saudi

Arabia with the same tactic by adding a notch.

The facts surrounding Khashoggi's death started swirling around at a rapid pace in the Turkish media and from there on the world media. Photographs of the fifteen-men hit squad were published and detailed flight information and CCTV coverage of their movements suddenly became available. Turkish reports were now published and leaked that Khashoggi had been dismembered and removed from the consulate in several parts inside body bags, fuelling further shock, embellishment and still some scepticism in the absence of physical proof.

'Turkish sources insist that Jamal Khashoggi was tortured, then killed and his body cut up,' tweeted Saudi whistleblower Mujtahidd, who had more than two million followers. 'All this was filmed and the video was sent to Mohammed bin Salman so he could enjoy the scene. If this is confirmed, then it seems like the news that he was removed from Turkey and has arrived in Saudi Arabia isn't true. Tomorrow Turkey should announce full details.'

The Turkish police did not go quite that far in public. However, a senior police officer leaked to the Qatari-funded news outlet *Middle East Eye* – for whom Khashoggi had written – that he was 'brutally tortured, killed and cut into pieces' inside the building. The source added that the attack was filmed in order to prove the mission had been accomplished.

Answers were required. Yasin Aktay told Qatari

broadcaster Al-Jazeera: 'We demand a convincing clarification from Saudi Arabia, and what the Crown Prince offered is not convincing.'

Mainstream Turkish daily newspaper *Hurriyet* also suggested that the Saudis had taken Khashoggi out of the building by cutting his body to pieces. The government mouthpiece *Sabah* offered further detail: 'The black minibus will explain the riddle of the Saudi journalist.... [It] left the building two hours after Khashoggi entered the mission.' This raised suspicions and the police were looking for it.

The waters soon got murkier with the Iranian channel IRTV1 (Iran is a close ally of Russia) reporting that Khashoggi's corpse had been found in a neighbourhood in Istanbul five days after he had disappeared.

Khashoggi's friend and Erdoğan adviser Yasin Aktay wrote in his column in *Yeni Safak*, another government mouthpiece: 'Although we are still trying to maintain optimism, we were not able to prevent the abduction or brutal killing of Khashoggi, whose ideas and stance I have followed with great appreciation and approval.... I know that all precautions have been taken.'

'We never had the opportunity to protect him, to do something when he was still alive,' he said. He and Khashoggi had talked the month before about the possible targeting of Saudi citizens. 'He voiced his concern about possible operations against Saudi citizens.... He was confident they couldn't conduct such operations in Turkey.'

The ultra-nationalist *Aydinlik* newspaper was more informed and alleged that Khashoggi was a spy and had brought 'significant documents' from Saudi Arabia.

'It is known that Khashoggi had left the country with several files containing secret information. Some of them are thought to be in Istanbul while others are in Washington,' it said.

Turkish government-mouthpiece *Yeni Safak* also added some conspiracy theories of its own by blaming the PLO, Israel, UAE, MBS, USA.

'The team and mentality that poisoned Yasser Arafat [the late chairman of the Palestine Liberation Organisation] to death is also behind the Khashoggi murder. Killers like Mohammed Dahlan [the former leader of Fatah in Gaza] are in the backstage. The Dahlan team studied Turkey a year before 15 July [Turkey's 2016 coup attempt] too! Although a journalist in opposition to Mohammed bin Salman has been killed, the signature belongs to Mohammed Bin Zayed al-Nahyan [the Crown Prince of Abu Dhabi and Deputy Supreme Commander of the United Arab Emirates Armed Forces]. He is Salman's patron. And the patron of both of them is US-Israeli intelligence.'

Nearly a week after Khashoggi had gone missing Donald Trump was now finally ready to address the issue as well.

'I am concerned about it. I don't like hearing about it. And hopefully that will sort itself out. Right now nobody knows anything about it, but there are some pretty bad stories going around. I do not like it,' the US president said, saying nothing in particular.

US Secretary of State Mike Pompeo called for a thorough and open probe by Saudi Arabia into Khashoggi's disappearance.

'We call on the government of Saudi Arabia to support a thorough investigation of Mr Khashoggi's disappearance and to be transparent about the results of that investigation,' he said in a statement. It was a polite way of saying, the US is not going to do anything, since the Saudis would not in a million years agree to an 'open' probe. Given a coy inside into US intelligence on the truth of Turkey's he added the vague words that he had seen 'conflicting reports'.

With the Khashoggi story having changed from missing to murder in the consulate, the speculation in anticipation of the facts changed dramatically.

'The Saudis are saying we can come investigate but they have, of course, disposed of the body,' said Aktay.

President Erdoğan, on a trip to Hungary, stirred the cauldron further. 'There are some people who came from Saudi Arabia,' he said. 'The public prosecutor's office is looking into the issue.' He added that CCTV footage from the airport was being studied.

Senior officials in Ankara leaked Khashoggi had been killed by a Saudi state hit squad sent to Istanbul to abduct or kill him. They were lying in wait when he arrived at the consulate on the afternoon of 2 October. Of particular interest were the convoy of six vehicles that left the consulate two hours after Khashoggi entered. Security camera footage showed boxes being loaded into a black van which carried diplomatic number plates. After leaving the consulate, three cars turned left on to a main road while the remaining three turned right. Investigators said one of the vehicles, a van with blacked out windows, had become the focus of the investigation. It had already been tracked to a nearby motorway where CCTV showed it taking the D100 expressway to Atatürk Airport, about an hour and fifteen's minute drive from the consulate.

The police traced one consulate-owned vehicle travelling to Belgrad forest north of Istanbul late that night, and another ninety minutes south of the city heading to the mainly rural Yalova province.

'Security forces have been examining footage from 150 cameras,' the privately owned website NTV reported. 'Two cameras which clearly see the consulate have been spotted. No footage was found regarding Khashoggi's exit from the consulate.'

The Turkish government were confident that the security cameras held the key.

'There were some vehicles,' said Yasin Aktay. 'There were fifteen Saudi personnel inside. They were carrying bags and going to the airport. Turkish security cameras can follow up until the airport.'

Two of the vehicles were of particular interest according to the Washington-based scholar Selim Sazak who had given the scoop on the Turkish charge of murder in the consulate and was now revealing more information leaked to him.

'One, on the suspicion that it might have been used to carry Jamal Khashoggi out of the consulate. Another, on the suspicion that it might have been used to shuttle some of the people involved,' he said, citing a briefing by Turkish officials.

The day after Khashoggi's disappearance, officials at the Saudi consulate were filmed burning documents in an oil drum in an open air courtyard by a drone operated by the Turkish authorities or an existing camera on a nearby building. They were destroying all paperwork concerning Khashoggi's murder, the Turks said. These included a 'killing order' brought from Riyadh on 1 October by a consulate work, it was said.

'He conveyed the order for the planned execution to consul general Mohammed al-Otaibi,' the pro-government *Sabah* newspaper reported.

In another line of investigation, the Turkish police were examining the flight records showing that two Saudi planes arrived at Istanbul's Atatürk Airport on Tuesday and departed separately that same day, hours after Khashoggi was last seen. While the Saudi authorities continued to insist they played no role in Khashoggi's disappearance, they now acknowledged that a 'security delegation' had been sent to Istanbul. But the Saudis did not offer a reason for the journey.

In Saudi Arabia, however, where MBS like Erdogan in Turkey, controlled the media and thus the story, the statements arising from the disappearance took a different turn.

The website of Saudi-funded Al-Arabiya TV said that the Khashoggi family were in contact with the Saudi authorities over his disappearance. Khashoggi's son Salah told the station diplomatically: 'The issue is that a Saudi citizen has gone missing. We are co-operating with the Saudi authorities to discover the circumstances of the incident....' Obligingly he added, 'The whole thing is a personal issue and is completely unrelated to politics.' Though US citizens, all of Khashoggi's sons had been placed under house arrest after the murder and were barred from leaving Saudi Arabia.

After chairing a family meeting in the Saudi city of Jeddah, legal counsellor Muatassim Khashoggi chipped in by publicly affirming his unwavering faith in the royal family: 'We trust the government and the measures it is taking. All efforts being exerted in Jamal Khashoggi's case are being coordinated with the authorities and the embassy in Ankara.'

He accused foreign media of using his brother's disappearance to 'attack our country for negative purposes'. In a script that seemed to underline one of the Saudi government's reasons for the assassination,

he said that they had never heard of Khashoggi's
'alleged' fiancée.

'We don't know her and we don't know where she
came from,' he said. 'She is not connected to the
family in any way. Her tales and her existence could be
part of her personal agenda.'

Salah Khashoggi backed this up: 'I don't know this
woman. I'd never heard of her before except from the
media.'

7
Horse-Trading

﹏

On 9 October, another key figured entered the fray. This was the Saudi ambassador to Washington, the Crown Prince's brother Prince Khalid. He had previously tried to persuade Khashoggi to return to Saudi Arabia. He now insisted that Khashoggi had not been detained, or killed by the Saudi authorities.

'I know that many people here in Washington and around the world are concerned for his fate, but I assure you that all reports saying that Jamal Khashoggi vanished in the consulate in Istanbul, or that the kingdom's authorities detained or killed him are completely false and baseless,' the diplomat said.

He did however confirm both Khashoggi's importance to the kingdom and the deep unease of Saudi top royals about the fact that he lived outside the kingdom: 'Jamal has many friends in Saudi Arabia, and I am one of them. Despite differences on a number of issues including what he called his "self-exile", we kept in touch when he was in Washington.'

Echoing the script recited by the Khashoggi family – under a travel ban to leave Saudi Arabia – Prince Khalid painted a picture of 'Jamal' as someone 'who has dedicated a large part of his life to serve his country'. The Ambassador went even further out on a limb. Like the consul general al-Otaibi he loyally called the rumours about Khashoggi's lethal fate 'malicious' and 'outrageous'.

On the same day, however, President Erdoğan's government launched another shot across MBS's bow. The Turkish press received more detail on the investigation into two Gulfstream jets owned by a company frequently used by the Saudi government landed in Istanbul the day Khashoggi 'vanished'. Marked HZ-SK1 and HK-SK2, the jets were reported to have come from Riyadh. According to pro-government *Sabah* newspaper, the former landed at 3:41am and the latter at 4:29pm. In all, fifteen Saudis converged on Istanbul for the covert operation. Nine people arriving on the first jet checked in at 5:05am for three days into the five-star Wyndham Grand Hotel as well as the less expensive five-star Mövenpick Hotel, both within walking distance if not eye line of the consulate.

Footage was leaked showing the elite team entering the consulate approximately thirty minutes before Khashoggi and leaving three quarters of an hour after he had entered at 1:14am. Among them were Kashoggi's friend intelligence officer brigadier-general Maher Mutreb, the leader of the operation, a thirty-one year old Saudi air force lieutenant called Meshad al-Bostani. On the outside CCTV footage that was leaked, furthermore, two civilians were seen entering the consulate as part of the team: Dr al-Tubaigy, head of forensic evidence of the Saudi Ministry of Interior and civil engineer Mustafa al-

Madani. Dr Tubaighy had come from the Mövenpick and Lieut. al-Bostani from the Wyndham Grand.

They all left within twenty four hours despite their three-day reservations, government-paper of record *Sabah* noted in its front-page scoop. Three Saudis arrived at Atatürk Airport on the second jet HK-SK2 at 4:29pm by which time Khashoggi had already been murdered. HK-SK2 took off for Riyadh via Cairo some two hours later taking some of the first wave of Mövenpick Saudis with it. The three Saudis of the second wave were young men in their 30s and they had also been booked into the Wyndham for three days. Despite arriving after the assassination they headed for the consulate and left the country 5 hours after arrival when HK-SK1 carried most of the remaining Wyndham Grand members of the fifteen-member team – flying first to Dubai and then Riyadh. Civil engineer al-Madani, however, left Turkey at 18 minutes past midnight on a charter plane, it was noted.

'They flew away with their secrets,' *Aksam*, yet another newspaper close to the government added. 'It seems that a period of headaches is about to begin for Saudi Arabia. A big crisis could break out between Ankara and Riyadh.' Hopefully it added, 'The horrible "extermination" of a journalist could also bring about the end of Crown Prince Salman.'

While the *Washington Post* published the last known photograph of Jamal Khashoggi – a still from the leaked CCTV footage showing him entering the Saudi consulate –Turkish officials said that if Khashoggi left the consulate he would have come out of the same door and would have been captured on the same camera.

Meanwhile, the BBC published off-air audio from an interview Khashoggi gave in London, three days before he disappeared. Asked if he would return to Saudi Arabia, he replied: 'I don't think I will be able to go home again. When I heard of an arrest of a friend who did nothing, it makes me feel like I shouldn't go. The people being arrested aren't even dissidents, they just have an independent mind.'

The BBC was criticised on social media for airing the recordings without Mr Khashoggi's consent and before there was any definitive proof of his death. This was particularly upsetting to Ms Cengiz. All she had to go on was leaked information by Turkish officials. Turkey had still not given an official account of Khashoggi's afternoon at the consulate.

'I no longer feel like I am really alive,' she said. 'I can't sleep. I don't eat. As his fiancée, as someone close to Jamal and in love with Jamal, I am waiting for information from my government about what has happened to him. Where is Jamal?'

To answer that question, the Turkish police said it had formed a 'special team'. They would look for DNA belonging to Khashoggi inside the mission, using Luminol and infrared light to find bloodstains, as well as 'K-9' police dogs in the search, they said. The

Saudi consulate promised its full co-operation and the ambassador said: 'What matters now is that the safety of Khashoggi is ensured and to reveal what happened.' But nothing happened.

This was for two reasons. On the hand, MBS wasn't going to let anyone have unfettered access. But also, behind the scenes, the Turkish government was negotiating furiously with Riyadh for horse-trading in a US-style deal: concessions in exchange for managing the intelligence it already had in its possession like it had with Washington – that is to say burying it.

Erdoğan's adviser Yasin Aktay helpfully wheeled back his earlier claim that his friend had been murdered and said in interview to *Russia Today* and quoted in Saudi's al-Arabiya that the 'the Saudi state is not blamed here', and even said 'we have our own deep state'. Though whether these were in actual fact Aktay's own words or ones edited by the Russian outlet is unclear. In any case, Turkey's willingness to do a somersault was finessed by government-paper of note *Sabah* which now once again speculated that Khashoggi might have been smuggled out alive on one of the two Gulfstream jets.

But MBS, having total state-control of the Saudi press, unlike the in the US or what was left of it in Turkey, was having none of it. He would not be arm-twisted like the US government into a mutually advantageous deal.

The Saudi press hit back like a well-oiled machine.

It was no longer Saudi enemies who were to blame but what they called 'international media campaign that did not verify the incident but relentlessly contributed to tarnishing the image of Saudi Arabia'. Reciting the usual verbiage of totalitarian regimes, it said the on-existent 'campaign' was 'politicised by sides that aim at settling scores with the kingdom at the expense of the truth'. The next day Aktay dismissed al-Arabiya's quote that Khashoggi could have been 'abducted by a third party, or perhaps by members of what he called the "deep state".' He blamed trolls for misquoting him.

Meanwhile (Shia) Iran's state-run Channel One thought it could kill two birds with one stone and reported that it was likely that Israeli agents had co-operated with (Sunni) Saudi Arabia in Khashoggi's murder.

Even Hatice Cengiz's optimism was dimmed by the deafening silence from her government.

'Although my hope slowly fades away each passing day, I remain confident that Jamal is still alive,' she said. 'Perhaps I'm simply trying to hide from the thought that I have lost a great man whose love I had earned.'

Writing in the *Washington Post*, she said her fiancé had told her that he missed his native Saudi Arabia and it had taken its toll on him. He had told her: 'I miss my country very much. I miss my friends and family very much. I feel this deep pain every single moment.'

When they were married, they would split their time between Washington and Istanbul. Khashoggi had already applied for US citizenship.

'We were in the middle of making wedding plans, life plans,' she wrote. 'After the consulate, we were going to buy appliances for our new home and set a date. All we needed was a piece of paper.'

'He had been feeling so lonely, but I could see the clouds clearing,' she added (unwittingly confirming to the Saudis how vulnerable Khashoggi had become, and that their intervention had been essential to safeguard the kingdom's secrets and relationship with Trump). Despite being worried about a wave of arrests in Saudi Arabia, she said, he did not fear anything happening to him on Turkish soil, saying he felt safe when he walked into the consulate and, no doubt, for being so close to President Erdoğan and his advisor Yasin Aktay whose number he had given to Hatice to call if something seemed wrong.

'I implore President Trump and first lady Melania Trump to help shed light on Jamal's disappearance,' she said. 'I also urge Saudi Arabia, especially King Salman and Crown Prince Mohammed bin Salman, to show the same level of sensitivity and release CCTV footage from the consulate.... Jamal is a valuable person, an exemplary thinker and a courageous man who has been fighting for his principles. I don't know how I can keep living if he was abducted or killed in Turkey.'

Later she wrote in *The New York Times*: 'Had I known it would be the last time I would see Jamal, I would have rather entered the Saudi consulate myself. The rest is history: He never walked out of that building. And with him, I also got lost there.'

Even though he had 'no foreboding of what was to come... He told me to alert the Turkish authorities if I did not hear from him soon.' Seemingly, he had little idea that he was risking his life. Her statement also indirectly twisted the knife into the US intelligence community. It had to defend itself why Khashoggi had not been warned.

'He was cheerful the morning we were going to the Saudi consulate,' she explained.

'We thought we would set the date of the wedding after dinner,' she said. 'This was part of the dream.'

But the dinner would never happen.

'Jamal and I are no longer in the same world,' she said. She raised the only question that was now left.

'The heart grieves, the eye tears, and with your separation we are saddened, my dear Jamal,' she tweeted in Arabic, also asking '#where is martyr Khashoggi's body?'

8

Dr Death from Glasgow

§

Now that Saudi Arabia had declined a deal the gloves came off. Turkish pro-government newspaper *Sabah* had already published the names of the fifteen suspects, also giving the year of their birth and printing pictures of all fifteen taken as they passed through passport control. They were all Saudi men aged between thirty and fifty-seven. The global press started filling in the CVs of the fifteen men. About Dr Salah Mohammed al-Tubaigy *Sabah* revealed more pictures showing that he was also on the board of the Saudi Society of Forensic Medicine and an expert in post-mortem examinations. The implication was – who better to clean up a crime scene?

The New York Times made the other connection and noted that he was a 'figure of such stature that he could be directed only by a high-ranking Saudi authority'. Al-Tubaigy had learnt his trade at Glasgow University, where he took a masters in forensic medicine, and he had spent three months with the Victorian Institute of Forensic Medicine in Australia. He was now being dubbed 'Dr Death'.

Other passengers were also being identified by the international and Turkish media. Taken together, the background information made clear that this was an elite Saudi hit squad of special forces members. There was a lieutenant colonel in the Saudi civil defence force; a major and lieutenant in the Saudi air force; a lieutenant in the service guarding the Crown Prince's palace; and team-leader Mutreb was quickly identified as a member of the Saudi intelligence community and former first secretary at the Saudi embassy in London. He was a former colleague of Khashoggi's at the embassy. They had been identified via open source internet tools by Oslo-based researcher Iyad al-Baghdadi. The Turkish daily newspaper *Sahab* also published a picture of one of them, royal guard Mohammed Saad al-Zahrani, hobnobbing with Mohammed bin Salman, while Mutreb was with the Crown Prince's entourage during his trip to the US in April 2018. The *New York Times* was to confirm their names and trace their closeness to MBS through its own research. CCTV coverage was leaked by Turkish officials showing Mutreb outside the Saudi consul general's residence on Meselik Street at 4.53pm.

CNN now identified Mustafa al-Madani, who was seen entering the consulate with forensic medicine chief al-Tubaigy arriving from the Mövenpick Hotel. The fifty-seven-year-old al-Madani was of a similar height and build as Khashoggi. He had allegedly been brought along as a body double, though – unlike Khashoggi – he did not have a beard coming into the building.

However, the masses of CCTV footage leaked by the Turkish authorities showed him wearing a fake beard when he left the consulate by a back door at

2.52pm, while Hartice Cengiz was waiting out front. He was then wearing Khashoggi's black jacket and had swapped his a blue-and-white checked shirt and dark blue trousers for Khashoggi's grey shirt and grey trousers.

'Khashoggi's clothes were probably still warm when al-Madani put them on,' a senior Turkish official said to CNN to provide grisly context.

However, when he emerged he was still wearing the same pair of dark trainers with a white stripe around the sole he had on when he entered the building, while Khashoggi had been wearing dark brogues. And while al-Madani had a full head of hair, Khashoggi was balding. CCTV showed al-Madani was accompanied by a man wearing a hoodie and a hooped shirt, and was carrying a plastic bag believed to contain the clothes al-Madani had worn when he entered the consulate. They hailed a taxi.

Half-an-hour later al-Madani was captured on CCTV at Istanbul's famous Blue Mosque in the Sultanahmet district. About half-an-hour after that, al-Madani and his accomplice entered a public toilet, emerging again at 4.22pm. al-Madani was then dressed in the clothes he wore when he entered the consulate, while the plastic bag his accomplice was carrying was now thought to contain Khashoggi's outfit. The two then had dinner in the Mesale restaurant, seemingly unperturbed by the events of the day. Then they took a taxi towards their hotel and threw the bag into a large bin nearby. They were later seen back at the hotel laughing and smiling. Al-Madani was to leave Turkey unhindered on a regular flight to Riyadh at 18 past midnight, back to safety in Riyadh – relative safety at any rate.

It remained unclear what had happened to Khashoggi's body, or body parts, though. Airport security officials said they checked all bags that the Saudi teams took with them when they returned to the airport. But, without its own ears in the consulate, Turkish intelligence was still in the dark what had happened to Khashoggi and the flight was treated as any other flight leaving from the airport. There was nothing suspicious in any of them and the bags were loaded on to the jets for their return journey to Riyadh. It later, in fact, transpired that the checks on the first plane were not as thorough as they might have been.

When the Turkish authorities, alerted by Khashoggi's fiancée, had become aware that Khashoggi was missing from his consular visit and the police rushed to Atatürk Airport, it had been too late to stop the first Gulfstream jet from leaving. But the second plane was still on the ground. It was searched and the authorities monitored the seven Saudis in the waiting room as they checked their luggage for the second flight. When nothing unusual was discovered, the private jet was also allowed to leave at 9:46pm, spiriting the military men of the operation to Saudi

Arabia safely – or so they imagined.

As assassination allegations mounted, the US government was obliged to say something as Khashoggi was both a US resident and a high-profile *Washington Post* journalist. The US script now started rolling. A statement from the White House said that several members of the Trump administration – John Bolton, the national security adviser, secretary of state Mike Pompeo and Jared Kushner, Donald Trump's son-in-law and senior adviser – had spoken to the Crown Prince by phone and asked for more details regarding the disappearance of the missing journalist.

Asked what advice he gave to MBS, Jared Kushner said: 'To be fully transparent. The world is watching.... Take this very seriously.' According to Kushner the Crown Prince's response was an off-hand, 'We'll see.'

'The reports that a Saudi-Arabian journalist may have been tragically murdered in Turkey should be deeply concerning to everyone who cherishes freedom of the press and human rights across the globe,' weighed in Vice President Mike Pence who could congratulate himself on the fact that the Khashoggi affair had proved to be the key to pastor Brunson's release. He promised Washington was ready to 'assist in any way' with the investigation. Given the US intelligence prior to the assassination, it wasn't quite clear what this assistance would really add up to.

'We cannot let this happen, to reporters, to anybody.' This surprising statement came was chipped in by Donald Trump in in an unusual reversal from his 'fake news' approach to members of the press. 'It's a very serious situation for us and this White House. I want to see what happens and we're working very closely with Turkey and I think we'll get to the bottom of it.' Saudi Arabia was also ordering $110 billion's worth of American weapons.

This didn't mean that the US government wasn't between a rock and a hard place. Leading Republican on the Senate Foreign Relations Committee Lindsey Graham said there would be 'hell to pay' if the Saudis had murdered Khashoggi. 'If this man was murdered in the Saudi consulate in Istanbul, that would cross every line of normality in the international community,' he said. 'If they're this brazen it shows contempt. Contempt for everything we stand for, contempt for the relationship.'

Senator Graham also blamed the Crown Prince directly, not holding his punches on Fox News: 'Nothing happens in Saudi Arabia without MBS knowing it. I've been their biggest defender on the floor of the United States Senate [but] this guy is a wrecking ball. He had this guy murdered in a consulate in Turkey, and to expect me to ignore it, I feel used and abused. The MBS figure is to me toxic. He can never be a world leader on the world stage. Saudi Arabia, if you're listening, there are a lot of good people you could choose, but MBS has tainted your country and tainted himself.'

A bipartisan group of twenty-two US senators signed a letter to Trump that triggered a US investigation and determination of whether human rights sanctions should be imposed over Mr Khashoggi's. The provisions for this mandatory investigation were in the Global Magnitsky Human Rights Accountability Act. This Act was one of the biggest eye sores of Vladimir Putin, as its broad injunctions against foreign individuals had been passed by US Congress further to the brutal killing of a Russian lawyer in Russian custody, trying to expose Russian corruption. It required the president to determine whether a foreign individual was responsible for a gross human rights violation. The act authorised the president to impose sanctions on foreign individuals 'responsible for extrajudicial killing, torture, or other gross violation of internationally recognised human rights against an individual exercising freedom of expression'. It was clear that the senators had MBS in their cross hairs, as well as his team of executioners.

'Our expectation is that in making your determination you will consider any relevant information, including with respect to the highest ranking officials in the Government of Saudi Arabia,' the letter said.

Asked about suggestions in Congress that arms sales to the kingdom be blocked, Donald Trump replied that such a move would hurt the US economy.

'Frankly, I think that would be a very, very tough pill to swallow for our country,' he said pouring oil on water. There was, of course, also the future of his own Trump businesses in the Middle East to consider after his presidency.

In Istanbul, the leaks meanwhile burbled on as President Erdoğan further opened the tap to put pressure on Saudi Arabia.

Turkish investigators turned their attention to the underground garage at the Saudi consul general's home where some of the cars that had left the consulate after Khashoggi's disappearance had headed. The mystery of the missing security camera footage at the Saudi consulate was also solved. Turkish authorities believe that the hard drive was removed when Turkish staff at the consulate were abruptly told to take a holiday on the day Khashoggi disappeared. They believed the footage was on board one of the planes carrying the assassination squad back to Riyadh.

US intelligence was also leaking some of its intel. The *Washington Post* cited American intercepts showing that the Crown Prince had ordered an operation targeting Khashoggi. The paper reported unnamed US officials saying the Saudis had been heard discussing a plan to lure the journalist from his home in Virginia and detain him. Several of Khashoggi's friends said that, over the past four months, senior Saudi officials close to the Crown Prince had called Khashoggi to offer him protection, and even a high-level job working for the government, if he returned to his home country, but Khashoggi had refused.

'There were offers made to Jamal to return from people close to the royal family, there were quite a few from Qahtani [MBS's Steve Bannon]. I don't think Jamal trusted him, he had a reputation,' said a friend. 'It is also the case that his divorce took place partly because his wife could not cope with the propaganda being aimed at him by the government, and Qahtani, of course, was running the propaganda against all who were considered enemies.'

How well-connected and important Khashoggi really was to Saudi Arabia all of a sudden became clear when it turned out that the Crown Prince – Saudi Arabia's ruler in all but name as his father was battling Alzheimer's – himself no less was thought to have made at least one of the calls to Khashoggi.

A few months before the murder, Khashoggi had also had the meeting with the Crown Prince's brother, Prince Khalid, the Saudi ambassador to the US, in what was described as a friendly meeting at the embassy in Washington where his return was also mooted. Khashoggi was visiting on a routine consular matter when he was summoned to Prince Khalid's top-floor office, where the pair spent roughly half an hour together. And Prince Khalid was only one among a number of Saudi officials who had been contacting Khashoggi, trying to persuade him to return, claiming he would be given a warm welcome and a high-level job. But Khashoggi feared he was being lured into a trap and would be imprisoned or worse, and decided not to return.

Saudi Arabia was not a good place to be for a writer. Reporters Without Borders said between twenty-five and thirty professional and non-professional journalists were being detained there in a country where there had never been press freedom. But, while Khashoggi was ostensibly friendly with President Erdoğan, Turkey was not at all a safe place for writers either. In fact, Erdoğan's record was worse than that of Saudi Arabia. According to advocacy group Sweden-based Stockholm Center for Freedom that tracks cases of prosecutions of Turkish journalists, Turkey had 245 journalists behind bars as of 24 January 2018, with another 140 journalists facing outstanding arrest warrants. Like Vladimir Putin from his election as Russian President 2001, Erdoğan had increasingly throttled the relatively free Turkish press since his first rise to power in 2003. Clearly there was more to the relationship between Khashoggi and Erdoğan than met the eye.

Initially Khashoggi had been informed that he could get his divorce papers from the embassy in Washington, but was then directed to the consulate in Istanbul as he intended to get married in Turkey.

'Jamal had been to the embassy in DC several times and they had dealt with his consular issues there,' said a friend. 'He thought he could get the documents he needed showing he was divorced, a legal requirement, from the people in Washington. I think they told him it was a simple matter. But then they said he needed to go to Turkey to get the papers. I am not sure whether he was told about going to Turkey by people in DC or Riyadh.' There seemed no reason for qualms at the time.

'It just seemed at the time to be a matter of bureaucracy. But now, after what has happened, there is obviously cause for suspicion,' the friend continued. 'Let's face it, they would not have dared to do what they did in Istanbul in America. They must have thought it would be much easier in Turkey to do what they planned.'

It was a good moment for Turkey to launch the next bombshell that had come into its possession.

Turkish officials now said they had an audio soundtrack of a blatant and brutal murder inside the walls of the Saudi consulate.

What was on the tape became the bedrock of the Turkish case against Saudi Arabia.

As the tape itself had not yet been leaked, attention turned to the question of how the Turkish authorities obtained the murder tape.

Turkish-government mouthpiece *Sabah* floated a theory that Khashoggi turned on his Apple Watch's recording facility before entering the Saudi consulate. Then his interrogation, torture and killing were recorded and sent to his iPhone, which was with his fiancée outside the consulate, and to Apple's iCloud. Experts determined what had happened inside the consulate from the material transmitted. Though this is technically feasible, it was thought unlikely and was merely a ruse to cover-up how the Turkish authorities had come into possession of the tape.

International speculation ranged from a bug placed in the consulate itself to a directional microphone focused on the building from outside – both technically within the realms of Turkey's capabilities. Another possibility, being discussed in Turkey and elsewhere (and more to the point given the fact that Turkey had seemed to be totally in the dark on 2 October and in the crucial first few days of Khashoggi's disappearance), was that some members of the hit squad recorded the abduction on their phones for trophy purposes and that those recordings were either intercepted in real time or retrieved from at least one of the killers' phones. Russia stayed well out of the discussion.

9

'Tourists'

ᕲ

Now that the Turkish government had dispelled any hope that Khashoggi was alive by leaking the existence of a murder tape, the media paused to consider the wider risks and perils of being a Saudi national. (Khashoggi's elite Saudi murder squad would have done well to take note.) Khaled bin Farhan, a Saudi prince living in exile in Germany, told the *Independent*: 'Over thirty times the Saudi authorities have told me to meet them in the Saudi embassy but I have refused every time. I know what can happen if I go into the embassy.'

Only two thousand out of some fifteen thousand princes control Saudi Arabia's wealth and Khashoggi was, due to his closeness to the inner sanctum, an insider. A run-of-the-mill prince would have even less protection than he had. They were privileged but essentially powerless individuals. Khaled bin Farhan added that there was deep anxiety among ordinary royals as to what had happened to Khashoggi.

'Around ten days before Jamal went missing they asked my family to bring me to Cairo to give me a cheque. I refused. Many, many princes are in jail right now in Saudi. Just five days ago a group tried to visit King Salman saying they were afraid for the future of the al-Saud family, they mentioned Mr Khashoggi's case. They were all put in jail.'

Khaled bin Farhan's story echoed the fate of another royal, prince Sultan bin Turki, grandson of Saudi Arabia's first king, Ibn Saud. He had vanished on the way Egypt in 2016 after criticising the Saudi regime.

'If I disappear you know what happened to me' was the last thing Sultan said to Bel Trew, the Middle East correspondent of the *Independent*.

Another of Sultan's friends said: 'I spoke to him before he got on the flight.... He actually joked that should he not make it, it was likely he was in Riyadh and I should raise the alarm.'

The prince was lured to Cairo, travelling on a royal private jet to see his father. But he was drugged and flown to Saudi Arabia instead. He was believed to be alive but under house arrest. His friends no longer have the means of contacting him. He had previously been kidnapped and drugged in Geneva in 2003 after calling for reform. Back in Riyadh he was held under house arrest and only returned to Europe in 2015 for medical treatment.

Saud bin Saif, a relatively minor prince who publicly backed calls for King Salman's removal, also went missing in 2016. Khaled bin Farhan thought Saud had been tricked into getting on a Saudi-owned private jet which, instead of landing in Rome, flew on to Riyadh. Prince Turki bin Bandar, once a major in the police who took to publishing videos criticizing the regime, disappeared in 2015 after applying for asylum in

France. Khaled bin Farhan believed both Turki bin Bandar and Saud may be dead. Ghanem al-Dosari, a Saudi satirist in exile in London, said he had not set foot in a Saudi embassy for nearly a decade, even though his passport expired in 2010.

'[The authorities] have a history of trying to lure people into embassies, they asked me to go inside the embassy in 2010 and I refused,' he said after Khashoggi went missing. 'I haven't travelled in years for fear of entering a country where I might be picked up. I know dissidents who are now scared to leave their apartments.'

While already oppressive, it seemed that the royal regime had shifted gears under MBS. Prince Abdulaziz, the forty-five-year-old son of the late King Fahd, allegedly disappeared in 2017 amid rumours he had been put under house arrest. Khaled bin Farhan said that Abdul-Aziz's family had no idea where he was, but they knew he was unwell. Also missing was Prince Khaled bin Talal, the fifty-six-year-old brother of Saudi billionaire al-Waleed bin Talal, who was arrested in December 2017. Royal family members said they have no idea where he was.

And in January 2018, Prince Salman bin Abdulaziz, an expert fencer and graduate of the Sorbonne, was called to the royal palace in Riyadh with some of his relatives. Soon after they arrived, a fight broke out between them and the bodyguards of the Crown Prince. The thirty-six-year-old Prince Salman was beaten unconscious. He has not been heard from since. His father, who was at the scene, was arrested two days later.

Non-royal Saudis were treated even more harshly. Ghanem al-Dosari, a London-based Saudi satirist, was attacked in a London street by two thought-to-be agents of MBS's regime. Dosari, who has refugee status in the UK, published footage of two men hitting him in the face in the Brompton Road on his YouTube channel that mocks the Saudi regime in August 2018. According to Dosari, they said: 'F*** London – the Queen is our slave.' He had received death threats in the past, including a threatening phone call, which he taped and published.

Major General Ali al-Qahtani, an aide to a senior Saudi prince seen as a potential rival to MBS, died in government custody after being detained in MBS's Ritz-Carlton shake-down of 200 leading Saudis. The *Daily Telegraph* reported that the general's 'neck was twisted unnaturally as though it had been broken' and that his body had burn marks which appeared to be the result of electric shocks. General Qahtani was taken to hospital, but was reportedly returned to his interrogation after being seen by doctors. The government has not offered an official explanation for how he died.

'People are very scared,' said a senior prince about the current situation. 'MBS is the reason people in my country are no longer sleeping.'

Days after the murder of Jamal Khashoggi, reports

came through that a journalist had been tortured to death in Saudi Arabia.

The authorities said Turki Bin Abdul Aziz Al-Jasser secretly ran a Twitter account called Kashkool, which exposed human rights violations by officials and the royal family in Saudi Arabia. He was arrested after Saudi moles in Twitter's regional office in Dubai unmasked him.

Amnesty International also reported that three female activists in prison in Saudi Arabia were subjected to electric shocks, torture, flogging and sexual harassment by officers.

One of the men accused was Saud al-Qahtani, the royal adviser to MBS and, as would be revealed later, the organiser of the murder of Jamal Khashoggi who had had a heated Skype call with him before he was killed.

For Saudi Arabia's friendly nations – whose citizens cannot be killed at will, or at any rate not without intercession of a criminal verdict – these allegations were a thorny matter.

In August 2018, Canada's foreign minister had tweeted her alarm at the imprisonment of the sister of a Saudi blogger Raif Badawi, who was himself in prison for 'insulting Islam through electronic channels' and sentenced to a thousand lashes. Riyadh announced a suspension of diplomatic ties, expelled the Canadian ambassador, declared a freeze on new investment and withdrew Saudi students from Canada. There was also concern about Salman al-Ouda, a religious scholar detained after refusing to tweet in support of the Qatar blockade and who may face the death penalty.

Meanwhile all was quiet on the Saudi front. It had still not granted access to the consulate to Turkish investigators as MBS had promised despite having 'nothing to hide'.

Quoting an official Saudi source, Saudi-funded Al-Arabiya TV however now reported that Riyadh 'welcomes the Turkish response to the request to form a joint team into Khashoggi's disappearance'. The source added: 'We trust the ability of the joint team... to carry out its mission. Saudi Arabia is concerned about the safety of its citizens.'

Meanwhile MBS's position in the kingdom remained unassailable. 'The bottom line is that the king has made it clear that despite the Khashoggi affair, he is not planning on removing his son,' a western diplomat told the *Sunday Times*. 'There is no group of people who are going to revolt against the king.'

Also MBS continued to be popular among ordinary Saudis who backed his social reforms. The killing of Khashoggi, a member of the Saudi elite and intelligence establishment, did not have a huge impact on them. The diplomat said: 'In Saudi they say they're sorry it happened but my wife gets to drive and I get to go to the movies.'

There would be some business consequences

though. Richard Branson froze business links with Saudi Arabia following Khashoggi's disappearance.

'I had high hopes for the current government in the Kingdom of Saudi Arabia and its leader Crown Prince Mohammed bin Salman and it is why I was delighted to accept two directorships in the tourism projects around the Red Sea,' he said. 'I felt that I could give practical development advice and also help protect the precious environment around the coastline and islands. What has reportedly happened in Turkey around the disappearance of journalist Jamal Khashoggi, if proved true, would clearly change the ability of any of us in the West to do business with the Saudi Government.'

'We have asked for more information from the authorities in Saudi and to clarify their position in relation to Mr Khashoggi. While those investigations are ongoing and Mr Khashoggi's presence is not known, I will suspend my directorships of the two tourism projects. Virgin will also suspend its discussions with the Public Investment Fund over the proposed investment in our space companies Virgin Galactic and Virgin Orbit.'

Branson also pulled of MBS's Future Investment Initiative conference in Riyadh – known as 'Davos in the desert' – along with World Bank president Jim Yong Kim, Uber chief Dara Khosrowshahi, Viacom's Robert Bakish, Steve Case, former head of AOL and Andy Rubin, the Silicon Valley entrepreneur best known for creating the Android smart phone operating system. Patrick Soon-Shiong, the owner of the *Los Angeles Times*, and *The Economist*'s editor-in-chief, Zanny Minton Beddoes, were no longer attending, and Arianna Huffington, the entrepreneur, media mogul and Uber board member, has also pulled out of the conference, having previously served on its advisory board. The *Financial Times*, *The New York Times*, Bloomberg, CNN and CNBC had withdrawn as media sponsors. Ford and JP Morgan also pulled out, along with government officials from the UK, US and other western nations where the media was not under state control.

Meanwhile, in an interesting echo of the Salisbury visit of the Skripal hit squad of the two Russian assassins, al-Arabiya baited the international media by saying that the fifteen-man Saudi security team whose pictures appeared in the Turkish press were, in fact, 'tourists'.

Turkish officials had no problem puncturing that balloon by providing the first details of the audio and video material and which proved that Khashoggi fell victim to this fifteen-strong elite team of assassins by whom he was grabbed as soon as he walked into consul general al-Otaibi's office.

'The voice recording from inside the embassy lays out what happened to Jamal after he entered,' said one Turkish official. 'You can hear his voice and the voices of men speaking Arabic. You can hear how he was interrogated, tortured and murdered.'

He was dragged from the Consul General's office into his study next door, where he was dumped on a table. Al-Otaibi himself could be heard saying: 'Do this outside. You're going to get me in trouble.'

'If you want to live when you return to Saudi Arabia, be quiet,' sneered Dr al-Tubaigy.

Khashoggi was held down as he was screaming in pain while this fingers were cut off – a punishment that the Crown Prince had warned would happen to those who criticised him. Khashoggi was injected with substance to silence him and throttled. Then there was a sudden silence.

An anonymous Turkish source told *Middle East Eye*: 'Tubaigy began to cut Khashoggi's body up on a table in the study while he was still alive. The killing took seven minutes.'

Further leaks to the Turkish press claimed the doctor directed the torture, using his expertise to administer drugs which would keep the Khashoggi conscious during the brutal interrogation, which saw his limbs cut off before he was decapitated.

The screaming only stopped when he was injected with an unknown substance thought to have been morphine. Dr al-Tubaigy then finished dismembering his body with a bone saw while Khashoggi was still breathing.

It was at this point that Dr al-Tubaigy told the others present, 'When I do this job, I listen to music.

You should do that too'. It drowned out the screams.

'There was no attempt to interrogate him. They had come to kill him,' another official source leaked to the Turkish press.

10
'Rogues'

ॐ

Thirteen days after Khashoggi disappeared, Turkish investigators were finally allowed into the Saudi consulate. Hours before a Saudi team of 'investigators' had done their preparatory job. They were really a cleaning crew who had set about their work with eight large bottles of floor-cleaning fluid along with other chemicals and six hundred bin liners, all delivered under the full glare of the TV cameras outside. The Turkish investigators arrived in a motorcade of six cars. The Saudi delegation entered the consulate an hour before Turkish police arrived and remained inside until the search was concluded.

The Turkish investigators were carrying no equipment after the Saudis had banned the use of Luminol, a forensic chemical that reveals bloodstains even if they have been washed clean. However, after an eight-hour search, they left with samples, including soil from the consulate garden. President Erdoğan suggested they found evidence of fresh coats of paint and 'toxic materials', but did not elaborate. One senior Turkish official leaked to the *Washington Post* there had been apparent attempts to scrub the scene and repaint areas, adding for the avoidance of doubt: 'People who have nothing to hide don't behave like this.'

Meanwhile the US script about Saudi Arabia continued. President Trump said that he had spoken to the ailing King Salman himself, who professed to having no knowledge about the missing journalist. Trump then speculated that 'rogue killers' may have been responsible for the murder. There had already be reports in the press that the Saudis were preparing to make a statement along these lines.

'Been hearing the ridiculous "rogue killers" theory was where the Saudis would go with this. Absolutely extraordinary they were able to enlist the president as their PR agent to float it,' retorted Chris Murphy, a Democrat senator.

The New York Times took up President Trump's theme. Information had been leaked to the paper that the Crown Prince had indeed approved the interrogation of Mr Khashoggi, or his rendition back to Saudi Arabia. But a member of its intelligence services, who merely happened to be a friend of the Crown Prince, had been 'tragically incompetent'. He had been trying to prove himself during the operation, which led to the journalist's death. The shift in the Saudi position had come after the US finally threatened sanctions against the kingdom.

Secretary of State Mike Pompeo flew out to Saudi Arabia to meet with King Salman and have dinner with the Crown Prince, ostensibly to have talks over Khashoggi's disappearance. On the same day, $100 million would be transferred from the Saudi coffers to the US Treasury, ringing up Donald Trump's demand on 2 October that Saudi Arabia should pay more for the US. President Trump also spoke to MBS on the phone. He tweeted: 'Just spoke with the Crown Prince of Saudi Arabia who totally denied any knowledge of what took place in their Turkish Consulate.'

Trump also defended Saudi Arabia from further criticism over the case, telling Associated Press with feeling that it was a case of 'you're guilty until proven innocent, I don't like that'.

It was noted though that Jared Kushner was conspicuous by his absence from the public platform. He had of course earlier been advising the Crown Prince on how to minimise the fallout from the Khashoggi disappearance by being transparent.

The rogue script that was agreed in the deal between the US and Saudi Arabia was now replacing the one where Saudi Arabia was 'disgusted' about the accusation of Khashoggi's assassination in the consulate.

Inside the kingdom those who only received Saudi media and didn't have access to foreign media were now thoroughly confused by the sudden concession by their government that Saudis close to MBS had after killed Khashoggi – and that it hadn't been done by foreigners.

In the early hours of 16 October, Khashoggi's younger son Abdullah tweeted a typed Arabic statement posted 'for immediate release', which the *Washington Post* picked up and published. It said: 'We, the children of journalist Jamal Khashoggi are following with growing concern the conflicting reports on his fate after we lost contact with him two weeks ago following his entry into the Saudi consulate in Istanbul.

This time the family once again loyally embroidered the new Saudi script of a rogue operation, 'The family is now trying to overcome the shock of the developments and gather all his children. Out of our moral and legal responsibility, we demand the immediate formation of an independent and neutral international committee to gather the facts into his disappearance and conflicting reports on his death.'

Just for the avoidance of any doubt, the message also reaffirmed both the honour of the Saudi government and the Khashoggi family name. 'Ultimately, the family calls on all sides to respect our privacy, particularly at this difficult time, and refrain from politicising his case and undermining his good reputation, which all people attest to.'

Two weeks after Khashoggi had disappeared from its consulate, Riyadh had finally changed its tune.

Rather than continue to maintain that Khashoggi had left the consulate in one piece, the way was now open for the Saudi government to follow King Salman and Trump's lead and blame 'rogue killers'. The official line now was that Khashoggi had been killed in the consulate after a fight broke out between him and the fifteen-man interrogation team, who had intended to take him back to Saudi Arabia. He died after being put in a chokehold, the Saudi government said. The team were then engaged in a cover up and employed a 'local collaborator' to dispose of Khashoggi's body. MBS knew nothing of this, in the new official Saudi script, though the person to be blamed was 'a Saudi intelligence official who was a friend of the Crown Prince,' *The New York Times* reported.

The New York Times then pointed out a glaring problem with the latest official story.

On 10 October it had reported information leaked to it by Turkish officials that Khashoggi was 'dismembered with a bone saw brought for that purpose'. Dr Salah al-Tubaigy, the specialist in gathering DNA from crime scenes and dissecting bodies, was with the interrogation team, along with his bone saw, it had reported further to the Turkish leaks. Clearly he was there for a purpose. He stayed late in Istanbul until 8:29pm that day, long enough to supervise the initial forensic clean-up of the consulate.

However, it might be convenient for both the US and Turkey to swallow this story, the newspaper added. Neither country was looking for a diplomatic confrontation and both countries had strong incentives to agree to a version of events that absolved Crown Prince Mohammed. One could see why MBS, Erdoğan, Putin and Trump disliked a free press.

On 17 October, Mohammed al-Otaibi, Saudi's consul general in Istanbul, was unceremoniously sacked and was placed under investigation over the

disappearance of Khashoggi. At least that is what
Saudi Arabia claimed. He flew back to Riyadh after the
UN urged Saudi to lift diplomatic immunity in the
investigation.

But where were Khashoggi's body parts? The story
circulated that his body had been dissolved in acid
after he had been murdered. A source close to the
investigation told Sky News that a 'very fast-acting
chemical' had been used. Meanwhile Turkish investigators were finally also allowed access to consul
general al-Otaibi's residence. Floodlights and a drone
were deployed in a search of the garden, because
Turkish authorities were not permitted to go into the
consulate's garden or to inspect the well in the
garden.

Jamal Khashoggi then found a voice from beyond
the grave. His last column, ostensibly submitted on
the day he went missing, was finally published in the
Washington Post on 18 October.

In a note with the column, Karen Attiah, the *Post*'s
global opinions editor, said the piece perfectly
captured Khashoggi's commitment to freedom in the
Arab world: 'A freedom he apparently gave his life
for.' The *Washington Post* had held off publishing it in
the hope that Khashoggi was alive and would return,
but with officials talking of rogue Saudi operators
and bone saws the intelligence services on all sides
had confirmed Khashoggi's demise.

'Now I have to accept: That is not going to

happen,' she wrote. 'This is the last piece of his I will edit for the *Post*.'

In the article, headed 'What the Arab world needs most is free expression', Khashoggi described how the optimism of the Arab Spring in 2011 was quickly dashed and replaced by the Middle East's version of an Iron Curtain, imposed by domestic forces as they grappled for power. The rest of the world had done little as journalists were arrested and newspapers silenced, he said.

'Instead, these actions may trigger condemnation quickly followed by silence', the column continued. 'As a result, Arab governments have been given free rein to continue silencing the media at an increasing rate....

'The Arab world is facing its own version of an Iron Curtain, imposed not by external actors but through domestic forces vying for power. The Arab world needs a modern version of the old transnational media so citizens can be informed about global events. More important, we need to provide a platform for Arab voices....'

'We suffer from poverty, mismanagement and poor education,' he wrote. 'Through the creation of an independent international forum, isolated from the influence of nationalist governments spreading hate through propaganda, ordinary people in the Arab world would be able to address the structural problems their societies face.'

With the US and Saudi script looking shaky on

account of the bone saw, suddenly more names from Turkish flight data started circulating on the hitherto unidentified members of the fifteen-strong assassination squad, leading to more background information on the team.

It became embarrassingly clear that almost all members were intimately connected with MBS's personal security and intelligence team. Among the new names was that of Abdulaziz Mohammed al-Hawsawi. A French colleague of his who had worked with the Saudi royal family told *The New York Times* that al-Hawsawi was a member of the security team that travelled with the Crown Prince.

Thaar Ghaleb al-Harbi was mentioned in Saudi media in 2017, when he was promoted lieutenant in the Saudi royal guard, apparently for his bravery defending the Crown Prince's palace in Jeddah during an attack.

Then there was Mohammed Saad al-Zahrani. A 2017 video by the Saudi-owned TV channel al-Ekhbariya published on YouTube showed a man wearing a royal-guard uniform and name tag standing next to the Crown Prince. At one, time he had also been on the embassy staff in London. A user with the same name on the Saudi phone-number app Menom3ay was listed as a member of the royal guard. A reporter from the *Washington Post* called the number and the man who answered denied having been in Turkey.

Walid Abdullah al-Shihri Shihri had been promoted major general in 2017 according to Saudi media. *Middle East Eye* had seen a document from the Saudi interior ministry listing him as a member of the Crown Prince's special security force.

Middle East Eye also identified Badr Lafi al-Otaibi as a colonel in the Crown Prince's entourage, who travelled with MBS to France in 2018, along with major Nayif Hasan al-Arifi, a security and protection support officer for the Crown Prince. On the number-sharing app, he identified himself as an 'employee of the Crown Prince's office'. A document seen by *Middle East Eye* also listed Mansour Othman Abahussain as a support officer for the Crown Prince. He was a brigadier.

Brigadier Abahussain, major al-Arifi and officer al-Zahrani were the three Wyndham Grand Saudis who had arrived after Khashoggi's assassination on the second private Gulfstream at 4:29pm. They seemed to be the sweep team, inspecting that every last detail had been attended to and charged with reporting back to Riyadh. They were to stay in Istanbul for as long as forensic crime expert Dr al-Tubaigy did and flew back with him on the Gulfstream that left Atatürk Airport at 9:45pm.

Fahad al-Balawi was listed as a member of the royal guard by two users on Menom3ay, while seven Menom3ay users identified Saif al-Qahtani as an employee of the Crown Prince. Khalid al-Otaibi also identified himself as a member of the royal guard. He travelled to the United States at the same time as official visits by members of the Saudi royal family. Hit-squad member Waleed al-Sehri was identified as an air force officer from an online video, while the facebook profile of Meshal al-Bostani said he was an air force lieutenant who lived in Jeddah and had studied at the University of Louisville, Kentucky. He died in a traffic accident at about this time and it immediately raised suspicions that he had been silenced by the Saudi regime in the crackdown on the team that had loyally executed the assassination order. Born in 1961 Mustafa al-Madani, Khashoggi's body double, was by some way the oldest of the group.

No information had been unearthed regarding the two other men who entered and left Turkey on 2 October. But they were now identified on new passenger lists by Turkish officials. They were Khalid al-Taibi and Turki al-Serei and were thought to have links to the Crown Prince, too.

At least three of the suspects – first lieutenant Dhaar al-Harbi, sergeant major Walid al-Shihri and Abdul al-Hawsawi – had been part of the MBS's entourage when he made a three-day visit to London in March 2018, where he met the Queen and Prime Minister Theresa May. Assassination squad leader, major general Mahir Mutreb, was also seen emerging from a car in Downing Street during the visit.

Despite the mounting weight of circumstantial

evidence, MBS still denied ordering the killing.

However, his officials were said to have privately conceded that Khashoggi died in the building at the hands of a rogue unit when 'an interrogation went wrong'. Who, then, was the culprit?

The prime suspect emerged as a two-star general new to intelligence work. He was going to be the designated fall guy in the latest Saudi script. According to the *Washington Post*, this was general Ahmed al-Asiri, deputy head of Saudi general intelligence directorate and one of the Crown Prince's right-hand men after MBS was made defence minister when his father came to power as king. A graduate of Sandhurst, West Point in the US, and St Cyr Academy in France, al-Asiri was a career air-force officer who came to prominence as spokesman for the Saudi-led coalition fighting in Yemen that had been unleashed by the Crown Prince as one of his first acts as Saudi defence minister.

In March 2017, al-Asiri was filmed sticking his middle finger up at protesters in London. This did not seem to damage his standing with the Crown Prince at the time.

Although he had no training in intelligence – to bolster the new cock-up script – it was said that he won the prince's permission to interrogate Khashoggi on the suspicion that Khashoggi was part of the dreaded Muslim Brotherhood, the Islamist political faction whose rise during the Arab Spring worried the Saudis and their allies in the United Arab Emirates.

The Saudis also wanted to intimidate Khashoggi for taking money from Qatar. According to the *Daily Beast*, 'the over-eager general exceeded bin Salman's intentions. He improvised a rendition to send Khashoggi from Turkey back to Saudi Arabia – and botched it, killing him. Then he lied to his Saudi superiors about what happened.'

How plausible was the new story?

'It's not going to wash,' said Bruce Riedel, a former CIA official and the Gulf expert at the Brookings Institution. 'It's ludicrous in the extreme. Saudi Arabia doesn't work that way. They don't do freelance operations.'

'If this is a rogue operation, the rogue is MBS,' said Barbara Bodine, a retired US ambassador to Yemen, knowing that if she said that as a Saudi citizen she would have signed her death warrant.

The Saudis must have been frustrated by the fact that people could freely talk back at the state, even if they had been former officials.

And then, of course, there was still the bone saw.

11
Technology

૭

Saudi Arabia officially admitted that Khashoggi was
dead. Khashoggi had indeed died in a fight in the
Istanbul consulate, but it was all a terrible mistake. In
a statement on state TV the country's public
prosecutor said that the fifteen-man squad confronted
Mr Khashoggi when he entered the consulate and the
brawl broke out.

To give the new script some teeth the public
prosecutor said that eighteen people had been arrested
in connection with his death.

The Saudi statement said: 'In implementation to the
directives of the leadership of the need to clearly
know the truth and declare it transparently whatever,
the preliminary investigations conducted by the Public
Prosecution showed that the suspects had travelled to
Istanbul to meet with the citizen Jamal Khashoggi as
there were indications of the possibility of his
returning back to the country.' The phrase 'indications
of the possibility of his returning' was mysterious. The
public prosecutor probably meant what usually results
when a gun is put to someone's forehead and he is
asked to return to Saudi Arabia.

'The results of the preliminary investigations also
revealed that the discussions that took place with the
citizen Jamal Khashoggi during his presence in the
Consulate of the Kingdom in Istanbul by the suspects

did not go as required and developed in a negative way, this led to a fight and a quarrel between some of them and the citizen Jamal Khashoggi, yet the brawl aggravated to lead to his death and their attempt to conceal and cover what happened.'

All fifteen men in the hit squad were arrested along with two consular staff and a driver. Saudi Arabia said the eighteen would be tried in Saudi courts. They had previously been described as tourists, though Saudi Arabia now conceded they were soldiers and intelligence operatives.

As if a legal wand had been waved, it was also revealed at the same time that the death penalty would be sought against five of the eighteen. No individual names, however, were given. And since the kingdom is hermetically sealed to the free press, there was no way of checking whether anyone had actually been arrested.

Furthermore, four other intelligence officials were also sacked, including general Ahmed al-Asiri, the deputy intelligence chief, and Saud al-Qahtani, MBS's Steve Bannon. Qahtani was viewed as Prince Mohammed's enforcer and had been considered untouchable by many Saudis. He was the one who had praised Khashoggi on the phone in his home in Virginia in 2017 for supporting MBS's initiative to let women drive, purring 'keep writing and boasting'.

Information was now leaked that a Skype call from Saudi Arabia to the consulate in Istanbul was made on

2 October after Khashoggi entered the building. During that call MBS adviser Saud al-Qahtani had begun to hurl insults at Khashoggi over the phone. According to the Arab and Turkish sources, Khashoggi answered Qahtani's insults with his own. Qahtani told his men to dispose of Khashoggi.

'Bring me the head of the dog,' he told them, though it remained unclear whether they did so apart from Khashoggi's fingers.

Critics of Saudi Arabia's new script pointed to several tweets by al-Qahtani as evidence that the Crown Prince was fully aware of the orders his aide was executing. In one 2017 tweet, al-Qahtani said: 'Do you think I make decisions without guidance? I am an employee and a faithful executor of the orders of my lord the King and my lord the faithful Crown Prince.' On the same day he warned a Saudi dissident living in London that the 'assassination file has been reopened'. Even after being sacked, al-Qahtani tweeted: 'I express my gratitude to the King and the Crown Prince for the great confidence they have given me and for providing me with the great opportunity to serve my nation over the past years.' He added: 'I will always be a loyal servant of my country.'

King Salman ordered MBS to head a committee to restructure the intelligence services within thirty days, either suggesting that the Crown Prince had been absolved of blame or that there was further covering up to be done.

'The kingdom has taken the necessary procedures to find out the truth,' the state news agency said, adding that the country's leadership had stressed 'the importance of knowing the truth clearly and announcing it transparently, whatever it is'.

Former MI6 chief Sir John Sawers said: 'All the evidence points to it being ordered and carried out by people close to Mohammed bin Salman.'

Pointing the finger at the US Sir John believed that MBS thought he had a 'licence' from Donald Trump, who frequently condemned journalists as the 'enemy of the people', even praising Republican Congressman Greg Gianforte for body-slamming *Guardian* reporter Ben Jacobs, saying 'he's my kind of guy'.

'I don't think he would have done this if he hadn't thought he had licence from the US administration to frankly behave as he wished to do so,' said Sir John. 'I think President Trump and his ministerial team are waking up to just how dangerous it is to have people acting with a sense that they have impunity in their relationship with the United States.'

Smoothly papering over the fact that Turkey seemed clueless on 2 October, former Whitehall mandarin Sir John also had his own theory as to where the tape the Turks had come from.

The theory didn't include Russia. Instead Sir John opined, 'There has been such tension between Turkey and Saudi Arabia over the last ten years or so they would have been monitoring very carefully what goes on inside Saudi offices.'

'They could well have had the consulate general bugged in some way or there may have been other devices carried by the squad which carried out the assassination which they were able to intercept.' Anything is possible, but Sir John's smooth theory wasn't corroborated by the facts. For four days, Turkey had been in the dark about Khashoggi's fate.

Another senior security 'source' chipped in to kill any further speculation about the loose end of the audio tape and video: 'Turkey launched a large-scale surveillance operation. Many in the intelligence community believe the consul was bugged, and this Saudi team was followed.'

Turkey, the 'source' suggested, had been taken by surprise. 'Turkey was expecting a rendition attempt, which they could interdict, rescuing Khashoggi. Instead, they witnessed a murder,' the source said. 'The uncomfortable truth may emerge one day that the hit team was listened to live as they killed Khashoggi, but [Turkey] was powerless to do anything about it.'

What was curious about the security 'source's' speculation was that it spectacularly failed to add up to the facts.

If Turkey had been listening in on what was happening in the consulate, it would have swung into action the moment Khashoggi's death throttle was heard while Dr al-Tubaigy wielded his bone saw and said he was decapitating and dismembering the corpse.

Turkish authorities would have grounded the two private jets, searched every inch of them as they lacked diplomatic status, and prevented the fifteen strong team from leaving Turkey, arresting all those who did not have diplomatic immunity and searching their luggage with a toothcomb and luminol. It would have given anything to thwart the success of the brazen assassination scheme by an arch-rival on Turkish soil. Anything less and the Turkish government would ook foolish in the eyes of the world in general, and its Middle-Eastern neighbours in particular – the disrespect MBS had shown Erdoğan by capturing a friend was beyond staggering.

The team and their luggage with sawn-off fingers, perhaps a head, and audio and video tapes would have been in Turkish hands without the world knowing what had happened. With the shoe firmly on the other foot, Erdoğan's leverage on Saudi Arabia would have been incalculable.

Quite apart from Turkish questionable intel prowess, it is inconceivable that the Turkish secret service listened in on the noisy assassination of a friend of their president's yet didn't act like lightening to control such an impudent operation once its perpetrators were outside the consulate.

Russian intelligence, however, does have the same technological capability and manpower as the US (as does China for that matter) to pick up chatter. If one looks at the 2016 US elections and UK Brexit

Referendum, Russia's deployment of technology may, in fact, be far superior. Unlike Turkey, where security-forces coups are common, it is also a country without divisive government factions that compete with one another. The Russian state used to be unified behind one holistic ideology but under Putin it is unified by the holistic pursuit of money. Furthermore, given Istanbul's vital importance to Russia's sea traffic, there is probably as much Russian-spyware cabling underneath its pavements as in Moscow.

Providing further padding to the script, Saudi officials also revealed that the kingdom had a general order on its books – presumably issued by no one else but MBS himself as crown prince – for Saudi dissidents to return home. The overly-keen general al-Asiri had wanted to impress MBS and acted on his own to plan an operation to capture Mr Khashoggi in Turkey, or so the story ran.

'There were no orders for them to kill him or even specifically kidnap him,' a Saudi official said for the avoidance of doubt that this was a white wash. 'Crown Prince Mohammed had no knowledge of this specific operation and certainly did not order a kidnapping or murder of anybody. He will have been aware of the general instruction to tell people to come back.'

It was just odd that the Crown Prince hadn't thought of mentioning this order in his Bloomberg interview on 3 October when asked whether Khashoggi was 'facing charges'.

Though of course, the word 'order to return' – if indeed that order had been 'general' – would likely have been misinterpreted by the six Bloomberg journalists who interviewed MBS.

12

'Physical Condition'

◌

While the blame game was being played out, Turkish authorities continued to expand their search for Khashoggi's remains. They claimed that 'after being loaded with several pieces of luggage, a minibus with the license plate 34 CC 1865 parked within the consulate grounds left the building around 3pm... for the consul's residence and believed that the bags held the remains of Khashoggi's dismembered corpse.

Using CCTV footage, they tracked hit-squad vehicles to the Belgrade Forest (a news outlet by Russia's ally Iran had already pointed in this direction), a large park on the city's northern outskirts, and to farmlands in Yalova Province about fifty miles from Istanbul on the other side of the Mamara Sea. A woman who lived there said that there had been more traffic than usual on the night of 2 October.

There were also calls for the Saudis to hand over the body, if they still had it.

The official Saudi script, however, now was that it had been carried out of the building by the rogue team. In an Agatha Christie Murder-in-Istanbul, they concealed it in a rug and had handed to a 'local collaborator' to dispose of, as if corpses were postage parcels to eternity. Even bad guys in movies about wartime Istanbul weren't that careless.

Official sources in Riyadh enthusiastically leaked

further details of the script. Among other things, it was said that the government wanted to convince Khashoggi to return to the kingdom from voluntary exile in America as part of a campaign to prevent Saudi dissidents from being recruited by the country's enemies. This addressed head on the fact that Khashoggi was a member of the Saudi intelligence community and did sound a lot closer to the truth.

So, the script went, general Ahmed al-Asiri, put together a fifteen-member team from the intelligence and security forces to go to Istanbul, meet Khashoggi at the consulate and tried to convince him to return to Saudi Arabia.

'There is a standing order to negotiate the return of dissidents peacefully, which gives them the authority to act without going back to the leadership' the official said, waving a legislative wand to make sense of it all. 'Asiri is the one who formed the team and asked for an employee who worked with al-Qahtani and who knew Jamal from the time they both worked at the embassy in London.'

The official said al-Qahtani had sent one of his subordinates to conduct the negotiations. According to the plan, the team would hold Khashoggi for some time in a safe house outside Istanbul, but would release him if he ultimately refused to return to Saudi Arabia.

Things went wrong from the start as the team overstepped al-Asiri's and al-Qahtani's orders and quickly employed violence, the official said. Khashoggi was ushered into the consul general's office where Maher Mutreb, brigadier general in MBS's intelligence detail, spoke to him about returning to Saudi Arabia. Khashoggi refused and told Mutreb that someone was waiting outside for him and would contact the Turkish authorities if he did not reappear within an hour. This was his fiancée, Hatice Cengiz and, a telephone call away, Erdoğan's advisor Aktay.

According to the official, Khashoggi told Mutreb he was violating diplomatic law and said, 'What are you going to do with me? Do you intend to kidnap me?'

Mutreb replied, 'Yes, we will drug you and kidnap you.'

The official also observed that Mutreb's words were an attempt at intimidation that, regrettably, violated the mission's peaceful objective.

When Khashoggi raised his voice, the team panicked. They tried to restrain him, placing him in a chokehold and covering his mouth, the official said.

'They tried to prevent him from shouting but he died,' the government account went on. 'The intention was not to kill him.'

Asked if the team had smothered Khashoggi, the official subtly shifted the cause of death on to Khashoggi's doorstep: 'If you put someone of Jamal's age in this position, he would probably die.' It was all a case of suffocation by age.

In an attempt to cover up what they had done in a

panic, the team had rolled up Khashoggi's body in a consular rug. Questioned, the Saudi officer would not give the nationality of the local man. And nor did the authorities know what this corpse collector had done with the body.

Forensic expert Salah al-Tubaigy then tried to remove any trace of the incident inside the consulate.

Meanwhile, operative Mustafa al-Madani donned Khashoggi's clothes, spectacles and Apple watch, and left through the back door of the consulate in an attempt to make it look like Khashoggi had walked out of the building.

The team then wrote a false report for superiors, saying they had allowed Khashoggi to leave once he warned them that Turkish authorities might get involved, and had promptly left the country before they were discovered. This explained the dramatic changes in the Saudi story. The team and three other local employees had been arrested and were under investigation.

Saudi foreign minister Adel al-Jubeir expressed his condolences to the Khashoggi's family, saying death was a 'huge and grave mistake' and promised 'to punish those who are responsible for this murder', although it was difficult to see how that job fall under the ministry of foreign affairs.

He told Fox News, President Trump's channel of choice: 'This operation was a rogue operation, this was an operation where individuals ended up exceeding the authorities and responsibilities they had. They made a mistake when they killed Jamal Khashoggi in the consulate and they have tried to cover up for it. That is unacceptable in any government. We are determined to uncover every stone. We are determined to find out all the facts. And we are determined to punish those who are responsible for this murder. Even the senior leadership of the intelligence service was not aware of this.'

Tut-tutting the global media's reaction to Turkey's leaks of the assassination and Saudi Arabia's somersault, he described the media outcry over the death of Khashoggi as 'hysterical'. Nonetheless, this could still be considered an improvement on the word 'disgusting'.

The Crown Prince himself called Khashoggi's oldest son to express his condolences as a sign of respect and who he was dealing with. MBS and King Salman later received Khashoggi's brother Sahel and son Salah.

Hatice Cengiz meanwhile complained that the Crown Prince never sent his condolences to her. The Khashoggi family, who claimed not to be aware of the whirlwind love affair, probably didn't mind.

'This incident, this assassination, took place inside a Saudi diplomatic mission,' she said. 'In such circumstances, the Saudi Arabian authorities are responsible for this.' There were fears for her safety and the Turkish authorities gave her twenty-four-hour police protection.

Only Egypt backed the new Saudi script. Like MBS, the el-Sisi regime hated the Muslim Brotherhood, founded in Egypt in 1928 (and whose conservative views had briefly appealed to Khashoggi in his youth). Briefly legalised after the Arabian 'Spring' by President Morsi – who owed his election to the brotherhood – it was once again illegal after Morsi's rule was overthrown a year later amidst popular protests against his attempts to replace the Mubarak era with an islamist one.

Few other nations found the new Saudi version of events credible, however. Even Donald Trump said he struggled with the Saudis' account, while the UK, France and Germany issued a joint statement saying there was 'an urgent need for clarification' on what happened inside the Istanbul consulate that day.

It was still the image of the bone saw that stuck in everyone's mind.

'You don't bring a bone saw to an accidental fistfight,' said Ben Sasse, a Republican congressman from Nebraska. 'The Saudis have said a whole bunch of crap that's not right, accurate, or true.'

Democrat Senator Jack Reed agreed across the aisles. 'This appears to have been a deliberate, planned act followed by a cover-up,' he said. 'You don't bring fifteen men and a bone saw to a fistfight with a sixty-year-old.'

Turkey wasn't letting the story peter out either. Turkish prosecutors did not accept the Saudi story.

'We have clear evidence that what happened in the consulate was planned in advance,' they said.

The Saudis had given the Turks details of the fifteen suspects and they had interviewed twenty-five employees of the consulate in Istanbul. However, Saudi Arabia's justice minister and chairman of its higher judicial council, Waleed al-Samaani, said that those responsible for Khashoggi's death will be tried inside the kingdom.

Turkey was seeking the extradition of the hit-squad, but it was now speculated that the hit-squad would simply be beheaded by the Saudis to prevent them from talking.

President Erdoğan snapped further at the heels of the Crown Prince, asking Saudi Arabia: 'Who gave the order for fifteen men to come to Turkey?'

Agnes Callamard, a UN spokeswoman on extra-judicial killings, also said the Saudi explanation was 'not plausible'. 'No government should accept it or the pretence at investigation,' she said.

Protesting outside the Saudi consulate, Turan Kişlakçi, the head of the Turkish Arab Media Association and a close friend of Khashoggi, summarised all questions that remained unanswered by Saudi Arabia with regards to the 'rogue' operation.

'Did they kidnap him? Where did they take him? How did they do this? These questions don't matter,' he said. 'There's only one thing that matters right now. Give Jamal back to us. Give him back so that we can raise his funeral. Let the whole world watch Jamal Khashoggi's farewell.'

On Monday 22 October Turkish state broadcaster TRT aired a new leaked surveillance video showing what Turkish security officials described as suspicious movement in a car park in Istanbul's Sultangazi neighbourhood. This included the image of a man moving a bag from one vehicle to another.

Turkish crime-scene investigators went to the car park in and found a grey BMW belonging to the Saudi consulate. It had been parked outside the consulate the day Khashoggi was killed.

The Saudis tried to prevent the Turkish police searching the diplomatic vehicle. But investigators, pressing ahead regardless, found two suitcases that contained Mr Khashoggi's personal belongings, including his laptop. They also examined the minivan belonging to the consulate and said they found Khashoggi's DNA in the back of it.

It was then suggested that body parts had been found in a twelve-metre well in the garden of the Saudi consul general's residence. Not only had the body been dismembered, but Khashoggi's face had been disfigured and the fingers were missing. They were said to have been flown back to Saudi Arabia to be presented to the Crown Prince as proof of the mission's success.

Nonetheless, speculation about Khashoggi's body continued with leaks saying that it had been dissolved in acid, possibly in the consul-general's garage. Family and friends in Saudi Arabia were still asking for its return so Jamal could be buried properly and they could mourn.

Sources leaked to the *Middle East Eye* that Prince Mohammed's bodyguard and leader of the operation, intelligence officer Maher Mutreb, was thought to have taken part of the journalist's body out of Turkey in a large bag. He had left on a private jet the day of the murder and his bags were not checked before the plane left Atatürk Airport. It was also revealed that Mutreb placed seven calls to the mobile phone of Bader al-Asaker, manager of the Crown Prince's private office, on the day of the murder, four times after the murder itself.

Khashoggi had written a number of articles critical of Saudi Arabia for the *Middle East Eye,* but not under his own name as he feared for his life. The *Middle East Eye* revealed that Khashoggi's assassins were members of a Saudi team of fifty highly-skilled intelligence and military operatives called the Firqat el-Nemr, or Tiger Squad and was well-known to foreign intelligence services. It had been formed more than a year earlier and operated under the guidance and supervision of Crown Prince Mohammed bin Salman.

The Turkish leak that body parts were said to have been found came on the same day as Khashoggi's brother Sahel and son Salah met King Salman and the Crown Prince at the royal palace. In a tweet, the foreign ministry shared a photograph of the men shaking hands with the caption: 'King Salman receives Sahel bin Ahmed Khashoggi and Salah bin Jamal Khashoggi in the presence of Crown Prince and share their deepest condolences and sympathy to the family of Jamal Khashoggi, may God rest his soul.'

However, according to the *Guardian*: 'They stared straight at each other, seemingly locked in the moment: the bereaved, Salah Khashoggi, had eyes of cold sorrow while the man offering condolences, Mohammed bin Salman, gazed back at him with steely focus.'

The meeting took place in the gilded office of the Crown Prince. Salah Khashoggi did not speak as they shook hands. But clearly discussions, though stiff, had been satisfactory for both sides. The ban on Salah, who holds joint US-Saudi citizenship, against leaving Saudi Arabia was lifted. He flew to Washington two days later with his family.

Meanwhile President Erdoğan stoked the fire once again personally. He reiterated that the hard drive of the consulate's CCTV system had been removed. Turkish officials had already leaked this information, but Erdoğan revealed that it had been done just before the gruesome murder, showing it was premeditated.

'We have strong signs that the murder was the product of a planned operation,' he told a rally of fans. 'This is a political killing.'

Erdoğan also insisted that the eighteen suspects be

tried in Turkish courts. However, that would not be enough.

'Leaving some security and intelligence forces holding the bag will not satisfy us or the international community,' Erdoğan said in a speech to ruling-party MPs in parliament. Oddly, the autocrat had refrained from such pronouncements in the case the nerve-agent poisoning in Salisbury that had led to the death of Dawn Sturgess and savage incapacitation of Sergei Skripal by Russia's secret *novichok* weapon. 'Saudi Arabia has taken an important step by admitting the murder. As of now we expect of them to openly bring to light those responsible – from the person who gave the order to those who carried it out – and to bring them to justice.'

He also promised that Turkey would reveal the 'naked truth' about Jamal Khashoggi's death. After all, the existence of a tape had been leaked – but not yet everything that was on it.

'All evidence gathered shows that Jamal Khashoggi was the victim of a savage murder,' he said. 'To cover up such a savagery would hurt the human conscience.'

President Erdoğan was again careful not to mention MBS by name or rank in his speech. But, Abdulkadir Selvi, whose *Hurriyet* (yet another newspaper of record for the Turkish government) columns were studied for indications of Mr Erdoğan's thinking, had no such qualms. He wrote, 'We cannot close this file until the Crown Prince is brought to account and removed from his post.'

Selvi also offered a new snippet of information from behind the baize door, Khashoggi had been cut into fifteen pieces and strangled slowly.

Donald Trump called the Saudi story 'the worst cover-up ever' and his administration put penalties on the conspirators. Among those sanctioned were Maher Mutreb and his team, but also Saud al-Qahtani, and consul general al-Otaibi. MBS, however, was not named as he was a friend of the administration and of the president's son-in-law.

Congress was not having it. MBS must have thought it most bizarre that the state didn't have the last word.

'We are putting all our weight behind the Global Magnitsky request,' said a senior Senate aide. 'We do not want to sanction the low-hanging fruit, we want to go as high as possible.'

Prime Minister Theresa May followed President Trump's lead and announced that the Saudi officials suspected of being part of the plot to murder Khashoggi would be barred from entering Britain. Again there was no mention of the Crown Prince whom she had recently met as an honoured guest.

It was not a very daring move as the men presumably had all been arrested in Saudi Arabia and, if not, would unlikely be allowed to leave the kingdom anytime soon.

It seemed that, privately, Saudi media were not

buying the government's account of Khashoggi's death either – though, of course, they wouldn't make any of their reservations public within the kingdom, least of all go on the record by name.

'People around me are feeling frustrated by this justification of it. They understand and know that everything, no matter how small, is ordered by the government. They don't buy it,' said one television journalist who worked for a pro-government station. He had worked alongside Khashoggi when he was a prominent media figure in Riyadh and was still in favour with the regime. Although the journalist had to peddle the official line on air, he said, from his knowledge of the Crown Prince, there is no way he would not have known.

13
'Pre-meditated'

જી

When the poorly attended Future Investment Initiative conference – Davos in the desert – kicked off on 23 October with many of the key participants missing, even the Crown Prince was absent from the opening session that morning.

He did turn up in the afternoon though. Bankers, corporate executives and Saudis stood as one to applaud in the ornate conference room when he finally arrived. But the applause was subdued compared to the thunderous ovation he had received at the Future Investment Initiative a year ago. Prince bin Salman spent only fifteen minutes at the event and left without giving his planned speech.

On the second day, he spoke to a packed auditorium, smoothly calling the murder of Khashoggi a 'heinous crime which cannot be justified' and vowing to bring the perpetrators to justice. Prince Mohammed called the death of the *Washington Post* columnist 'very painful for both the Saudi people and the world'. In an echo of the Bloomberg interview he gave the day after Khashoggi had been quartered and cut into fifteen pieces without mercy, he claimed that the barbaric assassination was being exploited with malice by some to drive a wedge between Saudi Arabia and Turkey.

'I want to send them a message: They will not be able to do that as long as there is a king called King

Salman bin Abdulaziz and a crown prince called Mohammed bin Salman in Saudi Arabia, and a president in Turkey called Erdoğan,' he said. 'Justice will be seen in the end.'

While MBS said the two countries would work together to bring all the perpetrators to court, he did not address accusations that he ordered the killing of one of his most prominent critics.

'He's not going to address the humungous elephant in the room, I bet,' one conference attendee, *Financial Times* Middle East correspondent Heba Saleh, had speculated before the Crown Prince gave his speech. Stunned silence met the first mention of Khashoggi's name, and a palpable relief followed. MBS's remarks received a short burst of applause, though the atmosphere remained subdued.

Alongside MBS on stage was Lebanese prime minister-designate Saad Hariri. MBS had been accused of kidnapping and roughing up Hariri the previous year, when Hariri didn't return from an official trip to Riyadh. During the visit former Saudi ally Hariri had then been forced to resign live from Riyadh after falling out over the growing Iranian influence in Lebanon.

The Crown Prince joked that Mr Hariri would only be staying in the kingdom for two days this time – 'so I hope you don't spread rumours that he was kidnapped,' he told the audience.

Hariri laughed nervously and applauded at this hilarious joke.

He had come back into favour after a leading Lebanese talk-show host was summoned to appear before Hariri in Beirut for making a joke at the expense of the Crown Prince. Associated Press reported that 'reacting to a clip on a rival network advising bin Salman to swear off fast food for his health, Haddad suggested he should swear off "fast arrests, fast politics ... fast military strikes", instead.'

Some delegates did not join the *folie à deux* and did little to hide their disdain for both the crime and the subsequent attempts to cover it up.

'These idiots have taken us back to the Stone Age,' said one. 'How do I defend this country to anyone anymore? The stupidity here is unparalleled.'

Others said the attempt to distance bin Salman from the slaying and blame it on his closest personal staff was doomed, but that they were forced to go along with it.

'It suits many of us to believe this, because the alternative is just too impossible,' said a Saudi businessman. 'But anyone who has lived here understands the fiction. And his friends outside cannot be expected to look away like us.'

Another said: 'This is very complicated. It is painful for the family and for the people. It is best to live in denial here.'

Abroad the Crown Prince's condemnation of the murder of Khashoggi was seen as disingenuous.

It emerged that, in the days following the assassination, MBS had told both Jared Kushner and US National Security Advisor John Bolton that Khashoggi was a dangerous Islamist and a member of the banned Muslim Brotherhood. It was a gambit that always worked wonders in the US.

'It will be harder under MBS to have the same degree of confidence we can work with Saudi Arabia in light of the brutal murder of Khashoggi,' said a former top western intelligence official – although it wasn't clear whether the word confidence applied to Congress not finding out about agreeable assassinations.

On 25 October, Saudi Arabia changed its explanation of Khashoggi's death yet again.

Now, it had no longer happened accidentally during a fistfight with rogue operatives. Yes, officials confirmed, the butchering operation had been planned. The Saudi attorney general Saud al-Mojeb issued a statement on state television, saying: 'Information from the Turkish side affirms that the suspects in Khashoggi's case premeditated their crime.'

The Saudi announcement came hours after CIA director Gina Haspel, while on a fact-finding trip to Turkey, had listened to excerpts from the audio tape which showed that Khashoggi was tortured before he was killed.

'The public prosecution continues its investigations with the accused in the light of what it has received and the results of its investigations,' the attorney-general said.

His new words were not taken very seriously either as Turkey alleged that an additional two members of the Saudi team had been sent to clean up the crime scene.

'We believe that the two individuals came to Turkey for the sole purpose of covering up evidence of Jamal Khashoggi's murder before the Turkish police were allowed to search the premises,' a senior Turkish official told the *Independent*. 'The fact that a clean-up team was dispatched from Saudi Arabia nine days after the murder suggests that Khashoggi's slaying was within the knowledge of top Saudi officials.'

Now that they were both out of the country, Khashoggi's two sons appeared to speak out a little bit more freely. They described their father as 'courageous, generous and very brave'. Thirty-five-year-old Salah told CNN: 'We just need to make sure that he rests in peace. Until now, I still can't believe that he's dead. It's not sinking in with me emotionally. It's not a normal situation, it's not a normal death at all. All what we want right now is to bury him in Al-Baqi [cemetery] in Medina with the rest of his family. I talked about that with the Saudi authorities and I just hope that it happens soon. It's an Islamic tradition. It's a basic humanitarian issue.'

Thirty-three-old Abdullah added: 'I really hope that whatever happened wasn't painful for him, or it was quick. Or he had a peaceful death.'

Asked how his father should be remembered, Salah said: 'As a moderate man who has common values with everyone... a man who loved his country, who believed so much in it and its potential. Jamal was never a dissident. He believed in the monarchy, that it is the thing that is keeping the country together. And he believed in the transformation that it is going through.'

The brothers also said their father was 'like a rock-'n'-roll star' when they were out with him in Saudi Arabia because of his career as a celebrated writer.

But in reality, their words about Khashoggi's (undoubted) belief in the monarchy etc. bolstered the Saudi government's latest script that this was all-rogue-gone-terribly-wrong.

The most significant new information was that his younger son now confirmed he knew Hatice Cengiz. In fact, he knew her rather well. Abdullah said his father's Turkish fiancée was making him happy. He was the last of Khashoggi's four children to see their father when he was alive. He said: 'We hung out in Istanbul. We had fun. I was really lucky to have a last moment with him. I feel very grateful.'

Despite the allegations that the Crown Prince had ordered the assassination, older brother Salah also reaffirmed his loyalty to the Saudi regime.

'The king has stressed that everybody involved will be brought to justice. And I have faith in that. This will happen. Otherwise Saudi Arabia wouldn't have started an internal investigation,' he said.

Khashoggi's two daughters, Noha and Razan, later paid tribute to their father in the *Washington Post*, vowing that 'his light will never fade'. They called him 'Baba – a loving man with a big heart' and chimed in with their brothers.

The put their finger on the mysterious reason for the assassination. 'In truth, Dad was no dissident. If being a writer was ingrained in his identity, being a Saudi was part of that same grain,' they wrote, emphasising his passionate love of his homeland. 'It was vitally important to him to speak up, to share his opinions, to have candid discussions. And writing was not just a job; it was a compulsion. It was ingrained into the core of his identity, and it truly kept him alive.'

They recalled their childhood, when the famous writer would allow them to rifle through his paper-stuffed office.

'We loved it when he took us every weekend to the bookstore,' they wrote. 'We loved looking through his passport, deciphering new locations from pages covered with exit and entry stamps.... As children, we also knew our father as a traveller. His work took him everywhere, but he always returned to us with gifts and fascinating stories. We would stay up nights wondering where he was and what he was doing, trusting that no matter how long he was gone, we would see him again, wide-armed, waiting for a hug. As bittersweet as it was, we knew from a young age that Dad's work meant that his reach extended far beyond our family, that he was an important man whose words had an effect on people over a great distance.'

They recalled visiting him in Virginia during Ramadan in 2017. 'Dad... told us about the day he left Saudi Arabia, standing outside his doorstep, wondering if he would ever return. For while Dad had created a new life for himself in the United States, he grieved for the home he had left. Throughout all his trials and travels, he never abandoned hope for his country.'

They returned to his home in Virginia after his death. 'The hardest part was seeing his empty chair,' they said. 'His absence was deafening. We could see him sitting there, glasses on his forehead, reading or typing away. As we looked at his belongings, we knew he had chosen to write so tirelessly in the hopes that when he did return to the kingdom, it might be a better place for him and all Saudis. This is no eulogy, for that would confer a state of closure. Rather, this is a promise that his light will never fade.'

Back in Saudi Arabia, the Crown Prince was trying to build up support in the ruling family by finally releasing Prince Khaled bin Talal, a nephew of King Salman, leading to speculation that other high-profile detainees would also be freed. Prince Khaled was a brother of billionaire investor Prince Alwaleed bin Talal, owner of The Savoy and Eurodisney, who had been temporarily detained in an anticorruption shakedown at the Ritz-Carlton in Riyadh. After Khashoggi's murder, the once flamboyant financier Talal dispensed effusive praise for Saudi Arabia's crown prince during a television interview, though he looked 'visibly uncomfortable', the *Financial Times* said.

His brother, Prince Khaled, had been held for eleven months in al-Hayer prison, south of the capital, with dissidents and activists for criticising MBS's reforms and his mass Ritz-Carlton detention of more than two hundred princes, ministers and businessmen held over allegations of corruption. Members of the royal family had been infuriated by the purge, which shattered decades of consensual rule, and the humbling of senior royals and powerful business magnates who were detained at the palatial five-star hotel.

Prince Khaled's belated release came days after the return from self-imposed exile in London of seventy-three-year-old Prince Ahmed, the king's younger brother who had been removed from succession. He was rumoured to be a possible replacement for MBS as Crown Prince. In a further attempt to limit the fallout from Khashoggi's murder, King Salman embarked on a week-long tour of Saudi Arabia, his first domestic tour since taking the throne in 2015.

The Crown Prince claimed that only eight people were still being detained from the Ritz-Carlton shakedown, but the *Washington Post* put the figure closer to forty five. Despite MBS's claim, oppression was not easing. New regulations were introduced to control the media. They were intended to protect public order, strengthen national unity, preserve the social fabric, and preserve values and virtues, the government said. Women working in media must also comply with Islamic dress codes.

MBS wants just 'one voice', said Yahya Assiri, a UK-based activist. 'In the past there could be some criticism with red lines for the media, but now there's just one line, one voice, repeating MBS and that's it,' he said.

Despite torture of Saudi guests at the Ritz-Carlton, Riyadh, its staff was named 'Hotel Team of the Year' and its general manager 'Highly Commended' at the 2018 Hotelier Middle East Awards held in Dubai.

Saudi Arabia itself was seeking to recruit London-based public relations agencies to rehabilitate its tattered international image.

14
The Tape

৯

Attempts to distract the world's attention from Khashoggi's murder were thwarted when President Erdoğan confirmed that recordings of the journalist's torture had finally been released to the UK, US, Germany, France and Saudi Arabia. It was another shrewdly calculated move to manipulate events in his favour. Like all authoritarian leaders, Erdoğan understood the incomparable power of the media as a herd management tool and was expertly skilled in stirring its cauldron.

For weeks, Turkey had been shelling Saudi Arabia's government with sickening snippets of its behaviour. Unlike Britain —supposedly a master in the art of diplomacy, Erdoğan had successfully forced the hand of MBS and made him look ridiculous. By handing over the recordings (though it was not clear whether all or just edited excerpts) he broadened the line of pressure on MBS. Landing a hot potato into the laps of the intelligence services of free-media countries, he ensured that the well-chewed out tape retained its media mystique and that it ended up in the hands of those who wouldn't be able to ignore it. They would now be giving their individual responses to the recording, keeping up the pressure on MBS.

President Erdoğan said: 'We played them to all who wanted them including the Saudis, the US, France,

Canada, Germany, Britain. The recordings are really appalling. Indeed when the Saudi intelligence officer listened to the recordings he was so shocked he said: "This one must have taken heroin, only someone who takes who heroin would do this".'

He also called on Saudi Arabia to identify the actual killer from among the fifteen-man team who had arrived in Istanbul before the murder.

'There's no need to distort this issue, they know for certain that the killer, or the killers, is among these fifteen people,' he said.

President Erdoğan, furthermore, put forward his preferred method of achieving this, 'Saudi Arabia's government can disclose this by making these fifteen people talk.'

Inevitably more detail of the assassination was leaked. Turkish newspaper of government record, *Sabah*, said it had heard the tapes and claimed that Khashoggi's words at the beginning of of torturing him were: 'I'm suffocating ... Take this bag off my head, I'm claustrophobic.'

Donald Trump confirmed that the US had the tape, but expressed little interest in listening to it.

'We have the tape, I don't want to hear the tape. There's no reason for me to hear the tape,' he said. 'Because it's a suffering tape, it's a terrible tape. I've been fully briefed on it, there's no reason for me to hear it. I was told I really shouldn't. It was very violent, very vicious and terrible.'

Others did listen to the tape and once again its contents began to leak. It was said that, soon after Khashoggi entered the consulate, he could be heard saying at the beginning of the altercation: 'Let go of my arm. Who do you think you are? Why are you doing this?'

'It was premeditated murder,' Turkey's foreign minister Mevlut Cavusoglu told Germany's *Sueddeutsche Zeitung* newspaper.

'It can be heard how the forensics expert instructs the others they should listen to music while he cuts up the body. One notices how he enjoys it. He likes to cut up people. It is disgusting.'

He added that the Saudi Crown Prince 'said he wanted the journalist silenced' – over 384 Turkish journalists in gaol or under criminal investigation saw their own reflection – and confirmed that Khashoggi was dead within seven minutes.

President Erdoğan said again that it was clear the murder had been planned and that the order had come from the top level of Saudi authorities. He also said could not think such a thing of King Salman, for whom he has 'limitless respect'.

On the day of the Khashoggi-sons' conciliation meeting with King Salman in October, the Turkish head of state had also gone out of his way not to embarrass the head of state of Saudi Arabia, his peer, and instead lauded King Salman's 'sincerity'. This was despite the fact that he had billed his speech on the day as the moment he would reveal 'the naked truth'. Erdoğan's speech didn't even confirm the existence of the murder-tapes, whose contents had already been widely leaked by then by Turkish officials.

It had been a diplomatic dance that was plainly aimed at unseating MBS (with whom both Jared Kushner and Donald Trump had exceptionally warm relations) from his all-powerful role in the kingdom, while not blaming Saudi Arabia as a country.

But on 13 November, for the first time, Erdoğan criticised MBS directly: 'The Crown Prince says "I will clarify the matter, I will do what is necessary". We are waiting patiently'. 'It must be revealed who gave them the order to murder.'

Foreign minister Cavusoglu revealed that the Crown Prince has asked to meet President Erdoğan at the forthcoming G20 meeting in Buenos Aires.

'At the moment there is no reason not to meet with the Crown Prince,' Mr Cavusoglu snapped. He added that Riyadh had offered to send identikit photos of local helpers who assisted in the cover-up.

'Why identikit pictures? The Saudis know the names,' he said. Indeed the names of most of the collaborators had of course already been leaked to the world by the Turkish government.

Others began putting the pressure on, too, for something to give.

Secretary of State Mike Pompeo phoned MBS to tell him that the US would 'hold all of those involved in the killing of Jamal Khashoggi accountable, and that Saudi Arabia must do the same', while British Foreign Secretary Jeremy Hunt brought the matter up with King Salman during a visit to Saudi Arabia. Saudi prosecutor general Saud al-Mujeb revealed that by now twenty one 'conspirators' were in custody – although it was not possible to verify what this meant in actual fact, given the prohibition of a free press in Saudi Arabia.

The prosecutor general now told a rare press conference in Riyadh that killers had set their plans in motion on 29 September, three days before Khashoggi was murdered and the day after he had first visited the kingdom's consulate in Istanbul. The deputy chief of Saudi Arabia's intelligence, general Ahmed al-Asiri, gave the order to repatriate Khashoggi, while the head of 'the negotiating team' brigadier general Mutreb that flew to the Istanbul consulate had ordered his killing.

'After surveying the consulate, the head of the negotiation team concluded that it would not be possible to transfer the victim by force to the safe location in case the negotiations with him to return failed,' the prosecutor said. 'The head of the negotiation team decided to murder the victim if the negotiations failed.'

Prosecutor general Saud al-Mujeb went on to absolve MBS, insisting that the crown prince had nothing to do with the operational cockup that led to Khashoggi's death. Everything had been done and dusted at the speed of a Saudi quill, and no wonder that King Salman duly praised the Saudi judiciary for exonerating his son.

However, the game of leaks to the media continued.

The New York Times reported that shortly after the assassination a member of the kill team said, in a hacked phone call – clearly not hacked by *The New York Times* itself but leaked – to his superior: 'The deed is done – tell your boss.' The words were uttered by hit-squad leader Mutreb and it was added that American intelligence officials believe 'your boss' was Crown Prince Mohammed bin Salman.

While Mutreb's former colleague was being slaughtered alive, at least three outside calls were placed by Mutreb and during the last one he said calmly 'Tell yours, the thing is done, it's done.' The word 'yours' in Arabic is taken to mean a senior or a boss. In addition to the videotaping of the whole thing so that Riyadh had proof that orders had been carried out correctly, Khashoggi's fingers would also be delivered as concurrent proof for al-Qhatani's chief that all had gone well.

While Mutreb's former colleague Khashoggi was being slaughtered alive, at least three outside calls were placed by Mutreb and during the last one he said calmly.

A Turkish newspaper also published leaked x-ray scans of the team's luggage, which included walkie-talkies, a signal jammer, electro-shock devices, scalpel blades, staple guns, long scissors and syringes. The bags were not opened due to diplomatic immunity, it said.

On 16 November the *Washington Post* report that the CIA had concluded that Crown Prince Bin Salman ordered the assassination of journalist Jamal Khashoggi. It was later leaked that Crown Prince Mohammed bin Salman sent at least eleven messages to Saud al-Qahtani, who was overseeing the operation, in the hours surrounding the murder. Qahtani was one of the officials who was sacked as part of the investigation by the Saudi public prosecutor and one of seventeen people sanctioned by the US Treasury Department who the US had linked to the killing. Again Saudi officials repeatedly denied that Mohammed bin Salman had any involvement.

Unofficially, a CIA official, however, told the *Post*: 'The accepted position is there is no way this happened without his being aware or involved.'

The agency had reached its conclusions after examining multiple sources of intelligence, including a phone call that the prince's brother, Khalid bin Salman, the Saudi ambassador to the United States, had with Khashoggi.

Khalid tweeted back furiously: 'I never talked to him by phone and certainly never suggested he go to Turkey for any reason. I ask the US government to release any information regarding this claim.'

Writing in *Hurriyet* – one of the Turkish newspapers to which Erdoğan's government preferred to leak – Abdulkadir Selvi also reported leaked information that the CIA had a recording of Saudi Crown Prince Mohammed Bin Salman giving instructions to 'silence Jamal Khashoggi as soon as possible' as the result of US wiretap. The Crown Prince and his brother Khalid were reportedly heard discussing the 'discomfort' created by Khashoggi's public criticism of the kingdom's administration.

How a Turkish paper would obtain CIA information was not at all clear, unless the CIA had leaked this titbit as a gesture of the new *détente* to the Turkish government and as a way to squeeze more money out of Saudi Arabia as Donald Trump had vowed in Mississippi on the day of Khashoggi's torture and dismemberment.

The Turkish newspaper also raised a new mystery: 'The hit squad, which was composed of close aides of Crown Prince Mohammed, told Khashoggi to send a message to his son, otherwise he "would be brought to Saudi Arabia." It suddenly hinted again at what Turkish ultra-nationalist *Aydinlik* newspaper had leaked in the early days: that Khashoggi was a spy and had brought 'significant documents' from Saudi Arabia.

Heightening the mystery, *Hurriyet* did not spell out what that message might be. Instead it merely stated that Khashoggi heroically rejected it, protecting his son, which 'led to the quarrel that ended with his killing by strangulation with a rope or plastic bag.' Completing the picture he had painted, Selvi wrote: 'The subsequent murder is the ultimate confirmation of this instruction.'

Despite the CIA's conclusions, President Trump himself refused to accept that the Crown Prince knew anything about the murder. No other president would similarly question his own government intelligence, but Donald Trump's presidency had started to depend on habitually undercutting executive parts of his administration.

'He told me he had nothing to do with it,' Trump argued with an eye on the long game of discrediting national security institutions. 'He told me that, I would say, maybe five times. He did certainly have people that were reasonably close to him and close to him that were probably involved.... But at the same time we do have an ally and I want to stick with an ally that in many ways has been very good.'

However, it was clear that, if the operation was sanctions by the Saudi government, MBS must have known about it. A western diplomat in Riyadh told the *Sunday Times*: 'He is the only real centre of power in the kingdom. There's no one that is seriously challenging him. And that also means there is no one else that could have ordered the murder.'

The US grew anxious about the growing gulf

between Turkey and Saudi Arabia, both important allies. It floated the rumour via the foreign press on 15 November that it was examining ways to expel Turkish cleric Fethullah Gulen, who Ankara says was behind a failed coup two years earlier, if Turkey toned down its criticism of the Saudi Crown Prince.

Throwing Gülen under the bus was the kind of proposal a reality show host might have come up with. The very last thing Turkey wanted was to have in its own backyard a widely-revered martyr who had triggered a recent coup. It would spell civil war. Holed up where he currently was in Pennsylvania, Gülen had become the Turkish poster child of US involvement in the coup. Erdoğan instantly squashed this cheap Big-Brother turn on the day.

Mourners gathered in mosques in Mecca and Istanbul though still no body had been produced and there was nothing to bury.

The mystery concerning its whereabouts deepened when this time one of Turkey's most senior politicians, defence minister Hulusi Akar, took up the matter and speculated that the killers may have taken the body parts out of Turkey.

'One probability is that they left the country three to four hours after committing the murder. They may have taken out Khashoggi's dismembered corpse inside luggage without facing problems due to their diplomatic immunity,' he said. If that is what Turkey knew for a fact, Akar came within an inch of telling Saudi Arabia what other information would be leaked in the future.

While the CIA said that MBS was behind the murder of Khashoggi, President Trump maintained that the jury was still out.

'Our intelligence agencies continue to assess all information, but it could very well be that the Crown Prince had knowledge of this tragic event,' he said. In a sly sideways move (perhaps in a stroke of Brunson's 'superhuman intelligence') he equivocated not on the facts known to the CIA, but rather on their sum total. He doubted whether these facts merited the CIA's conclusion beyond reasonable doubt: 'Maybe he did and maybe he didn't!… We may never know all of the facts.'

Having given his piece, Trump agreed to meet MBS at the upcoming G20 meeting in Buenos Aires, a city overlooked by a Trump hotel in Punta del Este. He was duly praised by MBS's friends in the Gulf States for his loyalty to the Crown Prince.

However, two senior senators again wielded the Global Magnitsky Act in an attempt to order the president to determine whether the prince was involved in the columnist's death.

'In light of recent developments, including the Saudi government's acknowledgement that Saudi officials killed Mr Khashoggi in its Istanbul consulate, we request that your determination specifically address whether Crown Prince Mohammed bin Salman is responsible,' they wrote.

'I disagree with the president's assessment. It's inconsistent... with the intelligence I've seen... The intelligence I've seen suggests that this was ordered by the Crown Prince,' Republican senator Mike Lee said on NBC's *Meet the Press*. Plainly he felt President Trump's assertion was at odds with the evidence.

'It is not in our national security interests to look the other way when it comes to the brutal murder of Mr Jamal Khashoggi,' Republican senator and former presidential rival Lindsey Graham concurred. 'Mr Trump has betrayed American values in service to what already was a bad bet on the thirty-three-year-old prince.'

Writing on Twitter, Bob Corker, chairman of the Senate Foreign Relations Committee added witheringly: 'I never thought I'd see the day a White House would moonlight as a public relations firm for the Crown Prince of Saudi Arabia.'

While Donald Trump continued to insist that the CIA had not found Prince Mohammed responsible and had come to no conclusion, Jack Reed, the senior Democrat on the senate armed services committee, put it more bluntly and said yes that the President was 'lying', foregoing the usual media euphemisms 'false statements'.

'The CIA concluded that the Crown Prince of Saudi Arabia was directly involved in the assassination of Khashoggi,' he said. Not only that, Reed added the

CIA had 'high confidence' in its assessment.

'It's based on facts, it's based on analysis,' he said. 'The notion that they didn't reach a conclusion is just unsubstantiated. The CIA has made that clear.'

The unanimous US senate resolution stated that Saudi Crown Prince Mohammed bin Salman was responsible for Khashoggi's murder and it formally withdrew US support for the Saudi war in Yemen (that MBS had started).

In response to this senate resolution, the Saudi foreign ministry released a statement saying: 'The recent position of the United States, which has been built on baseless allegations and accusations, includes blatant interference in its internal affairs and the role of the kingdom at the regional and international level. The kingdom has previously asserted that the murder of Saudi citizen Jamal Khashoggi is a deplorable crime that does not reflect the kingdom's policy, nor its institutions, and reaffirms its rejection of any attempts to take the case out of the path of justice in the kingdom.

'The kingdom hopes that it is not drawn into domestic political debates in the United States to avoid any ramifications on the ties between the two countries that could have significant negative impacts on this important strategic relationship.'

Though he would have been a more plain if not crude, Vladimir Putin couldn't have improved upon this statement.

Mevlut Cavusoglu, the Turkish foreign minister,

summarised the situation saying that Trump was turning a blind eye to the murder. He then lashed out at the EU's response, which he complained was no more than 'cosmetic'. Given Turkey's own free-press record, he was more used to having to defend himself.

Emboldened by the senate's accusation of MBS as the assassination's king pin, Erdoğan said, 'We have learned this from the audio recordings: of those who arrive, those closest to the Crown Prince played the most active role,' said President. 'The perpetrators are clear to me.'

Citing Nikki Haley, outgoing US envoy to the United Nations, taking the same line as the senate, President Erdoğan said, 'She openly named people'. He couldn't believe his luck with the democratic US, 'This shows something. Now, the whole incident is fully resurfacing.'

He added: 'It's clear where this business will end up.' Though it wasn't entirely clear where 'where' was.

It was a small wonder that, two weeks later, government-mouthpiece newspaper *Safak* would on 31 December 2018 crown President Erdoğan 'the world's most prominent leader' for its Turkish readers.

15

High-fives in Buenos Aires

ও

Before travelling to the G20 in Argentina on 30 November, MBS visited the United Arab Emirates, where he met his closest ally, Crown Prince Mohammed bin Zayed of Abu Dhabi, the country's *de facto* ruler. He would go on to Gulf state Bahrain, Egypt and Tunisia, all thought to be friendly allies sponsored by Saudi Arabia, on his way to Buenos Aires. The tour sent a clear message to the world that the Crown Prince's position remained unassailable in the kingdom. It was King Salman's equivalent of saying, I am not considering to install any rival in the royal family, and it is safe for MBS to be out of the country.

Nonetheless, when MBS landed in Tunisia there were popular protests. A large banner hanging from the headquarters of the Tunisian journalists' union showed the prince wielding a chain saw – a reference to the dismemberment of Khashoggi's corpse. Demonstrators carried placards saying, 'The murderer is not welcome' and 'Go away assassin', while some held up hacksaws.

'It's inhuman to see an Arab leader killing his brothers in Yemen, and the murder of a journalist is the icing on the cake,' said Basma Rezgui, a teacher brandishing a red-stained bone saw.

'He's a very dangerous person because he doesn't

seem to understand politics or respect his own people or other people,' said Radwan Masmoudi, president of Tunisia's Centre for the Study of Islam and Democracy, who was among those protesting MBS's visit. 'There's no way he'll bring stability. His actions speak louder than his words.'

Meanwhile, the location of Khashoggi's body remained an unresolved topic and a fertile source for creating new headlines. Despite earlier unofficial reports that Khashoggi's body parts had been found in the garden of the Saudi consul general's garden, the Turkish police now also searched a palatial villa the size of MBS's own French chateau near the town of Termal in the Yalova province near Istanbul.

It belonged to Mohammed al-Fawzan, a Saudi businessman close to MBS. On 26 November, Istanbul's chief prosecutor had added his name to the roster of the Saudi hit squad, saying al-Fawzan had spoken on 1 October to Mansour Abahussain who was on the three-strong sweep team that arrived on the second plane after Khashoggi's assassination.

'The chief prosecutor's office believes that this phone call was about disappearing or hiding the body parts of the murdered journalist Jamal Khashoggi,' the official press statement said. Mr al-Fawzan was not in Turkey when Mr Khashoggi was killed, but Turkish investigators believed he may have let the hit squad use his property – though there was no suggestion that al-Fawzan personally knew of the assassination or that the hit squad might try to hide the body at his property. Large photographs of King Salman and the Crown Prince adorned the walls inside the villa.

Investigators clad in white suits with blue gloves and show covers took a particular interest in a well on the grounds of the villa, which they drained and in which they said they found traces of chemicals. They used drones and dogs in the ten-hour search, which covered the grounds of a neighbouring property. The prosecutor said al-Fawzan, codenamed 'Ghozan', had been called by Mansour Abahussain, the Saudi officer of the Crown Prince's security detail who had been arrested by Saudi authorities along with other members of the hit squad.

'Jamal Khashoggi's body was cut into pieces and dissolved after his murder in the Saudi consulate in Istanbul,' said the prosecutor's press release. 'As a part of the ongoing investigation, it has been detected that the day before suspect Mansour Othman got in touch with Saudi citizen Mohammed Ahmed in Yalova. It is assumed that their conversation is connected to the Khashoggi murder, and the dissolving and hiding of his body.'

The prosecutor also noted that a man named Fawzan Mohammed Ahmed al-Fawzan had been appointed head of a Saudi company shortly after the Crown Prince seized control of it from one of the rich Saudis he imprisoned on corruption charges at the 2017 Riyadh Ritz Carlton shakedown.

In Buenos Aires, Human Rights Watch submitted papers calling on Argentina to use a clause in its constitution to prosecute MBS for the murder of Jamal Khashoggi and war crimes in Yemen if he attended the G20. A file containing details of Khashoggi's slaying and other cases of torture was sent to the prosecutor's office. Argentina's constitution recognises universal jurisdiction for war crimes and torture. This means the authorities can investigate and prosecute those crimes no matter where they were committed. The Argentine prosecutor did accept the request to prosecute Mohammed bin Salman, but when MBS arrived in Argentina, he was warmly received by government officials nonetheless.

On the brink of the summit, the US senate had reached for a new measure to overrule President Trump's foreign policy. They voted to end their support for Saudi Arabia's war in Yemen in response to the murder of Jamal Khashoggi. The move, significantly, was not partisan and had the support of both Republicans and Democrats. Following a briefing by CIA director Gina Haspel, leading senators also said plainly that the Saudi Crown Prince was 'complicit' in the killing of Jamal Khashoggi.

Senate foreign relations committee chairperson Bob Corker told reporters: 'I have zero questions in my mind that the Crown Prince directed the murder... If he was in front of a jury he would be convicted in thirty minutes. Guilty. So, the question is what do we do about that.'

Senator Lindsey Graham, concurred, saying: 'There's not a smoking gun, there's a smoking saw. You have to be wilfully blind not to come to the conclusion that this was orchestrated and organised by people under the command of MBS and that he was intricately involved in the demise of Mr Khashoggi. I think he is complicit in the murder of Mr Khashoggi to the highest level possible. I cannot support arm sales to Saudi Arabia as long as he's in charge.'

When the G20 summit opened in Buenos Aires on 30 November, Prime Minister Theresa May said she would confront the Crown Prince about the killing of Jamal Khashoggi. They shook hands, at any rate, in a firm and steady way. A Downing Street spokesman said: 'The Prime Minister stressed the importance of ensuring that those responsible for the appalling murder of Jamal Khashoggi are held to account, and that Saudi Arabia takes action to build confidence that such a deplorable incident could not happen again.'

French President Emmanuel Macron also had a word. MBS told him not to worry about the Khashoggi murder.

'I am worried,' Macron had replied. 'You never listen to me.'

'I will listen, of course,' MBS replied. 'It's OK. I can deal with it.'

But the most significant meeting was between

President Putin and MBS.

Putin had grown up in Soviet Russia at the height of its power and had been stationed in as Komissariat-5 KGB officer in East Germany where the Stasi held files on over one third of the total population. MBS, unlike most Saudi royals, had never lived abroad. Both authoritarians shared the view (with Erdoğan) that the national media was merely a crowd-management tool of the population at large. The point of a free press was entirely incomprehensible to both men, who merely saw it as an irritant that got in the way of their will.

Putin was well-seasoned in flouting international opinion since his rule began in 2001. Like MBS he had started out being the darling of the global media, hailed as a breath of fresh air – that is, until the excruciating death by poisoning of former FSB colonel Alexander Litvinenko, in London, with rare isotope Polonium 210 produced in a high-security Russian government facility. He had merely shrugged his shoulders indifferently at the fall-out, gleefully countering what was levelled at Russia with his own 'facts' and 'conclusions' in a precursor to Trump's rallying cry of 'false news'. Since then he had invaded and incorporated Crimea as part of Russia, fired on Ukranian boats in the Kerch Strait, all without real punishment.

He had literally got away with the assassination of many inconvenient people outside of Russia, notably in Britain (Dr Matthew Puncher, the scientist who identified Polonium 210, strangely committed suicide after a visit to Russia) and even some in the supposedly safe US. One of his latest casualties was Dawn Sturgess, who had tragically died of the poison intended for fellow Salisbury-resident, the former GRU colonel Sergei Skripal. Skripal had survived the debilitating attack. Nothing of note had happened to Russia that deterred it. Putin had even tilted at the US presidential elections through Facebook and Twitter without any real repercussions to speak of – certainly not under President Trump's White House, which was fearful that an investigation would by extension question the legitimacy of his presidency.

In fact, when Putin had launched his surprise attack on 'traitor' Sergei Skripal at the energy conference on 3 October, the day after Jamal Khashoggi had been disfingered, decapitated and dismembered by Saudi operatives, Putin helpfully summarised his own experience with the fall-out of international opinion for his listeners – who included Saudi Arabia representatives. Dismissing it as 'hubbub', he concluded that it would always die down eventually. The real problem on the other hand Putin thundered was: 'As is well known, espionage, like prostitution, is one of the most important professions in the world. Nobody has managed to stop them and nobody is still able to do it.'

Two days before the G20, the Kremlin had promised that a face-to-face meeting between MBS and Putin where they 'would discuss the killing last month of Saudi journalist Jamal Khashoggi... oil markets and the conflict in Syria'. They could now discuss directly what Putin had previously said at the two energy conferences.

How would this meeting go? Since 2 October, Putin had drawn Saudi Arabia's rival Turkey closer with the taped information on the Khashoggi murder, and Putin had further successfully destabilised Washington. Russia was the third largest oil producer in the world. Saudi Arabia was at the fulcrum of global opinion due to the tapes. How, then, were relations with fellow oil producer Saudi Arabia and MBS, head of Aramco, the world's second largest oil producer after the US?

More than excellent, since you ask. All was clearly forgiven. Like school boys in on a racket they high-fived and it was all smiles. President Donald Trump, sensing no publicity opportunity, appeared to snub them both, on this occasion.

16

Questions

૭

A trove of text messages between Khashoggi and Montreal-based activist Omar Abdulaziz surfaced in December. They showed the depth of Khashoggi's animosity to MBS. One read: 'Like Pac-Man... the more victims he eats, the more he wants. I will not be surprised if the oppression will reach even those who are cheering him on.' Another called the ruler who had never lived outside the kingdom a 'beast'. According to the *Independent*, the texts may have been accessed by Saudi security officials and contributed to the plot that led his death.

It was claimed that Khashoggi was preparing a social media protest against the regime before he was murdered. He and Abdulaziz outlined plans to post documents detailing human rights abuses carried out by Saudi Arabia and spread the information via the tweets of young Saudi dissidents, CNN reported. Khashoggi pledged $30,000 towards the plan, which included sending untraceable foreign Sim cards to activists in Saudi Arabia. After Khashoggi's death, Abdulaziz sued NSO Group, an Israeli software company that he believed provided spyware to the Saudis, allowing the government to hack their messages which were conveyed via the normally secure WhatsApp.

Khashoggi was also at the heart of an 'online

army' of Saudi activists fighting a misinformation cyberwar, according to friends who feared he may have been targeted because of his support. He had recently given $5,000 to 'Geish al-Nahla', or the Bee Army, an opposition movement offering cyber protection to Saudi activists needing a safe platform to speak out inside the oppressive kingdom. This was also the brainchild of twenty-seven-year-old Omar Abdulaziz.

Turkey also took action. An Istanbul court issued arrest warrants for former deputy head of Saudi intelligence general Ahmad al-Asiri and Saudi royal court adviser Saud al-Qahtani for 'wilful murder with monstrous sentiment'.

'The prosecution's move to issue arrest warrants for Asiri and Qahtani reflects the view that the Saudi authorities won't take formal action against those individuals,' a Turkish official said. But Saudi Arabia made it clear it would not extradite the suspects.

'We don't extradite our citizens,' said Saudi foreign minister Adel al-Jubeir.

UN human rights chief Michelle Bachelet agreed and called for an international investigation. On 30 January, while UN investigator Agnes Callamard was in Istanbul, Saudi Arabia had still not agreed to give access to the consulate. Callamard was allowed to listen to the tape. In Washington, DC, protestors renamed the street outside the Royal Embassy of Saudi Arabia 'Khashoggi Way'. Their fake street sign was accompanied by an inflatable rat made to mimic Donald Trump.

More damaging to the White House, it was reported that Jared Kushner offered private counselling to Mohammed bin Salman on how 'how to weather the storm' after the murder. Three former senior US officials said the private exchanges could make him susceptible to Saudi manipulation. Kushner urged his hotelier father-in-law to stand by the Crown Prince, which indeed he did. The Saudi prince then boasted to his counterpart in the United Arab Emirates, Crown Prince bin Zayed, that Kushner was 'in his pocket'.

Time magazine named writer Jamal Khashoggi and three persecuted journalists as its 'Person of the Year'. The three were Maria Ressa who was the co-founder of Filipino news site *Rappler* and had criticised President Duterte's anti-drug crackdown which had killed nearly five thousand people since 2016, and Reuters reporters Kyaw Soe Oo and Wa Lone who were arrested in Myanmar on 12 December 2017 while investigating the execution of ten Rohingya men. They had been sentenced to seven years in prison.

If the leaks are true, the Saudi team also made a video tape of Jamal Khashoggi's last moments so that Riyadh had proof that its orders had been carried out correctly. And Khashoggi's fingers were delivered as concurrent proof for al-Qahtani's 'yours' that all had gone well and that the elite team had executed their orders with military precision.

To date, Jamal Khashoggi's remains have not been located. We are also left with the question whether he was murdered because of his opinions or because of what he knew about Donald Trump as a member of Saudi's top intelligence community. And to what extent US intelligence closed its eyes...?

None of the facts in this book, except for the facts provided by Jamal Khashoggi's fiancée Hatice Cengiz, would have been known if the intelligence services of the countries involved had not decided to leak or counter-leak facts in their possession. We would still be entirely in the dark. She herself would always have harboured the niggling doubt that Jamal might surreptitiously have left her standing there.

And so, unless there is another Edward Snowdon or Chelsea Manning out there willing to risk their lives or imprisonment, it is unlikely that we'll ever have answers that aren't manipulated for a purpose other than the truth. New revelations will follow, but only if one or more of the security services involved think an objective may be achieved to their benefit.

Appendix

Tuesday October 2
The Saudi Consulate
Istanbul (GMT +3)

3.13 am	*Gulfstream jet with tail-mark HZ-SK1 lands at Atatürk Airport from Riyadh carrying between nine and 15 passengers*
1.14 pm	*Jamal Khashoggi is pictured on CCTV entering the consulate*
3.30 pm	*The consulate closes with no sign of Khashoggi, according to his fiancée*
3.45 pm	*Six vehicles, including two vans with blacked-out windows, leave the consulate*
4 pm	*Khashoggi's fiancée alerts the Turkish authorities*
5.15 pm	*A second Gulfstream jet with tail-mark HZ-SK2 from Riyadh lands at Atatürk Airport*
6.20 pm	*It then takes off for Egypt, before returning to Riyadh*
10.46 pm	*The first jet is searched by police and takes off for Dubai, before also heading on to Riyadh.*

Tuesday October 2
Southaven, Mississippi (GMT -6)
Rally for Senator Cindy Hyde-Smith

'You have to pay.'

DONALD TRUMP: We protect Saudi Arabia. Would you say they're rich? And I love the king, King Salman. But I said 'King – we're protecting you – you might not be there for two weeks without us – you have to pay for your military. You have to pay'... They have got to reimburse us.

Wednesday October 3
Moscow (GMT +3)
Russian Energy Week 2018

'*A traitor.*'

VLADIMIR PUTIN: Watching some media outlets, I see that some of your colleagues are pushing forward the theory that Mr Skripal is almost some kind of human rights defender. He is simply a spy, a traitor to his homeland. You get it? There is such a thing – a traitor to one's homeland. He is one of them. [Applause!] Imagine: You are a citizen of your own country, and all of a sudden you have a man who betrays his own country. How will you, or any representative of any country sitting here, look at him? He's simply a scumbag, that is all there is to it.

rferl.org/a/putin-slams-traitor-sergei-skripal-bastard/29523407.html

Wednesday evening October 3
Riyadh (GMT +3)
MBS interview with Bloomberg

'I would know that.'

Bloomberg: What's the Jamal Khashoggi story?

MBS: We hear the rumors about what happened. He's a Saudi citizen and we are very keen to know what happened to him. And we will continue our dialogue with the Turkish government to see what happened to Jamal there.

Bloomberg: He went into the Saudi consulate.

MBS: My understanding is he entered and he got out after a few minutes or one hour. I'm not sure. We are investigating this through the foreign ministry to see exactly what happened at that time.

Bloomberg: So he's not inside the consulate?

MBS: Yes, he's not inside.

Bloomberg: Turkish officials have said he's still inside.

MBS: We are ready to welcome the Turkish government to go and search our premises. The premises are sovereign territory, but we will allow them to enter and search and do whatever they want to do. If they ask for that, of course, we will allow them. We have nothing to hide.

Bloomberg: Is he facing any charges in Saudi Arabia?

MBS: Actually, we need to know where Jamal is first.

Bloomberg: So he might be facing charges in Saudi Arabia?

MBS: If he's in Saudi Arabia I would know that.

Bloomberg: So he's not the person mentioned by Saudi Press Agency?

MBS: No, definitely not.

October 18
Sochi (GMT +3)
Valdai Discussion Club

'I hope America will not go as far as Saudi Arabia did.'

Ragida Dergham: Thank you, my name is Ragida Dergham.
I am Founder and Executive Chairman of Beirut Institute.
It's a think tank for the Arab region with a global reach...
On Saudi Arabia, of course, the world is preoccupied with the
developments, and I'm wondering what consequences or... Do
you see that there may be consequences, on your particular
relationships, Russian-Saudi relations, given that you have
been eager to have good relations and beyond.

VLADIMIR PUTIN: Now concerning Saudi Arabia.
What is it that is bothering you? I can't understand.
We have built really good relations with Saudi Arabia
in recent years. Please, specify your question about
Saudi Arabia. What is it that is perplexing you in this
regard? Why should our relations with Saudi Arabia
break down?

Ragida Dergham: As you know, because of the developments
in Istanbul, at the Saudi Consulate, there is a big interest
worldwide in the investigation regarding the assassination or
the killing of Jamal Khashoggi, the journalist who was our
colleague and has been a participant in the Valdai Group. So
this is what I am talking about. Right now, of course, there is

pressure on President Trump that may reflect on the mid-term elections, and there are countries pulling out and countries being concerned, I mean, media and others are concerned about continuing to be present in Saudi Arabia given the alleged feeling that maybe someone in the government may be involved in this atrocity, of killing of Jamal Khashoggi. That is what I meant. Do you think it will impact your relations with Saudi Arabia at all?

VLADIMIR PUTIN: As far as I know, the journalist, who has disappeared and whom you have just mentioned, lived in the United States of America. He lived in the US, not in Russia. In this sense, the US, of course, bears certain responsibility for what has happened to him. This goes without saying.

He was the one to go to the United States for asylum. In this connection, I would like to say the following. First, we should wait for the results of the investigation to become available. How can we, Russia, start spoiling relations with Saudi Arabia while being unaware of what has really happened over there?

As far as I can judge, this man was to a certain extent a member of the Saudi elite. In some way or other, he was connected with certain ruling circles. It is hard to say, what is going on there.

But we can see that complicated processes are also taking place within the US elites. I hope America will not go as far as Saudi Arabia did. But we don't know what, in fact, has happened over there. So why should we take any steps directed at downgrading our relations, if we do not understand what is really happening?

If someone understands it and believes that a murder has been committed, then I hope that some evidence will be presented and we will adopt relevant decisions based on this evidence. This gives me a pretext to say something else.

From time to time, there are steps taken against Russia and even sanctions are imposed, as I have repeatedly said, on the basis of flimsy excuses and pretexts. They groundlessly claim that we have allegedly used chemical weapons, even though, incidentally, we have destroyed our chemical weapons, while the United States has failed to do so despite the obligation to that effect it assumed.

So, there is no proof against Russia but steps are being taken. According to claims, the murder was committed in Istanbul, but no steps are being taken.

Uniform approaches to problems of this kind should be sorted. To reiterate: Our policy towards Saudi Arabia has evolved over a long period of time, over many years. Of course, it is a misfortune that a man has disappeared, but we must understand what has really happened.